# Message from
# a Blue Jay

# Message from a Blue Jay

## Love, Loss, and One Writer's Journey Home

### Faye Rapoport DesPres

Buddhapuss Ink LLC • Edison NJ USA

Cover Art based on *Bird Nest* @ Elena Ray / Dreamstime.com
Cover and Book Layout/Design by The Book Team
Copyediting by Andrea H. Curley
Author photo by Bill Chapman
Library of Congress Control Number: 2014933743
ISBN 978-0-9842035-2-9 (Paperback Original)
First Printing May 2014

Some essays in this collection have previously appeared in the following:
"The Diversion," in *Writer Advice*
"Up to Nothing," in *Hamilton Stone Review*
"Forty-Six," in *Ascent*
"No One Watches the Old Lady Dance," in *Connotation Press: An Online
Artifact*
"The Bird's Nest," in *Damselfly Press*
"The Deer," in *Eleven Eleven*
"Into the Vacuum," in *Prime Number Magazine*
"Waiting for the Hurricane," in *Platte Valley Review*
"Tulips," in *Superstition Review*
"Survivors," in *TOSKA Magazine*
"Morning and Night," in *Sugar Mule's Women Writing Nature Issue*
"Walden Revisited," in *Connotation Press: An Online Artifact*

Some names and identifying details have been changed by the Author to
protect the privacy of individuals.

To my husband, Jean-Paul Des Pres,
and
my parents, Benzion and Gloria Rapoport.

## From the Author

Imagine arriving at a train station in the middle of nowhere. On your lap lies a suitcase, and in that suitcase you carry your past. Metal brakes screech, the train slows and stops, and you struggle as you carry the suitcase toward the door and down the stairs to the platform. The whistle sounds, and the train pulls away as steam rises from the tracks. You survey the landscape beyond the station and think: *Where am I? What now? What happens next?*

This is how I arrived at what I call my "middle decade," the decade between forty and fifty. The suitcase I carried was heavy with memories—not just recollections of my youth and adulthood in America, but also inherited memories from an immigrant family splintered by the events of World War II. Born against a backdrop of displacement, loss, and ultimately hope, I was raised in upstate New York. Over the years I moved from New York to Boston, to England, Israel, Colorado, and eventually back to Boston. I gathered life experiences as if they were pieces of a puzzle and hoped, without realizing it, that those pieces would eventually form some kind of whole. In retrospect I can see that my desire was to find what many of us seek: love, a sense of peace, and a home.

The essays in my book emerged from the pieces of that puzzle that inspired—or haunted—me most. They were crafted in an effort to fashion a big picture from the fragments of a restless life. I examined events in both the present and the past, the history of my family, the start of a second marriage the same year my mother-in-law's life was drawing to a close, body image, aging, and the passage of time, and the connection I have always felt to animals. I explored these things while at a stage of my life where I had seen a lot of things but still had—as I have now—a great deal more left to see.

You will meet colorful characters (some human, some not), visit places from Canada to Bermuda and the Middle East, and witness the conflict between the desire to examine one's life and the ultimate need to let go of it all in order to live in the moment. Perhaps you will find, as I did, that the natural world and the creatures who inhabit it—from a humpback whale to an astonishing blue jay—can provide insight in unexpected ways.

Soon I must prepare for the next part of my journey. Which of these memories should I pack up and which should be left behind? There's just enough time to rexamine them while I wait for the train to pull away from the station. The future is waiting. Care to join me?

~ Faye

# The Deer

I am with my father in his small white skoda, a Czechoslovakian import rarely seen in the United States. I am young, a teenager. My father is a large, powerful man. We are driving on County Route 5, not far from the house where my family lives in upstate New York. Darkness surrounds the little car as it hums along the road. There are no streetlights in the countryside, so the black night is uninterrupted except by our headlights, which cast two cones of light straight ahead, revealing small sections of the road as it twists through the shadowy landscape.

It happens in an instant.

A deer darts out from nowhere. The animal's body seems to fill the entire windshield. It tries to leap across the road, but we are too close and too fast. There is a terrible jolt, a loud bang as we hit the deer. My father cries out; his voice is strangled. A moment passes. I am frozen, petrified. The car has stopped in the middle of the road, but the engine is still running. I turn my head toward my father. He is sobbing.

The memory of that moment many years ago—when my father hit the deer—flashes in front of me when I least expect it. Sometimes it comes to me when I am working at my desk or in the middle of lunch at a restaurant. Sometimes I see it when I am lying quietly in bed in the middle of the night.

Usually when the image appears, I rapidly shut it out. I see the headlights, I see the deer, I hear the loud bang, I feel the jolt, I hear my father's anguished sob. I see his head hanging forward on his chest as he gasps and sobs. And then I push the image as far away from conscious thought as my mind will allow, because I am afraid.

There are many details I don't remember. I don't recall exactly how old I was when the incident occurred. I don't know where my father and I were going on that deep, quiet night. I know the skoda, which my father loved, was badly damaged. It was repaired at a local car shop, and my father eventually passed it on to my brother. One day, years later, my brother passed it on to a young mechanic from the town garage, who completely restored it. He smoothed the dented fender and hood and painted it bright red.

But the memory is not really about the car.

When I am feeling brave, I try to understand what the memory *is* about. In those moments I don't push it away. I see the headlights, I see the deer, I hear the loud bang, I feel the jolt, I hear my father's anguished sob. Then I try to stay with it. I let in as much as I can, for as long as I can take it. I try to face the fear.

What circumstance led me to be riding in the car with my father that night? Was I happy to accompany him? While I was growing up, my father left us for four days every week to work as a psychotherapist in New York City. His office also served as his apartment. My mother raised my brother, my sister, and me in an old farmhouse surrounded by forty acres of fields, located two and a half hours north of the rest of my father's life. The family only felt complete when he arrived home each Friday, and I ran to him, eager to share my childhood troubles and successes.

But his moods could turn from loving warmth to rage in

an instant, and without warning. Small things would set him off; I remember him slamming his fist on the table one night when my mother forgot to set out a saltshaker at dinner. He would scream at the three of us over unintended infractions and send us to our rooms in tears. Once he kicked our beloved German shepherd when the dog did not obey him. Then the moment or the mood would pass, as quickly as it had come on, and my father would regret his behavior. He would call to us, forgive us, hug us close, fold us tightly against his chest, reel us back toward calm.

I don't want to give the wrong impression when I say my father kicked the dog. A few years ago, when he was well into his seventies and began to slow down with the onset of Parkinson's disease, my father told me that kicking the dog was one of the things he deeply regretted when he looked back at his life. He loved that dog. He simply couldn't control himself when he was enraged. He once picked up a coffeemaker and threw it against the kitchen wall during an argument with my mother. But he was never physically abusive to her, or to us. He loved us; he loved animals. Although the walls of our farmhouse were busy with the scratching and scraping of field mice, he never bought mousetraps or poison. In fact, he would panic if a mouse appeared in the room, not because it was there, but because he was afraid one of the cats would catch and kill it.

More than once he caught the mouse himself, opened the door to the backyard, and dropped it gently outside. He always said he hoped it would be safer there.

Perhaps I was happy to be invited to ride with my father that night. I might have felt special because he was paying attention to me or wanted to spend time with me; maybe he had offered to transport me to a school event or to a party in a neighboring town. When I think about being in the car, in the moments before we hit the deer, I sense that I was installed cozily in my seat, surrounded by the endless, dark night, feeling safe with my father beside me and the headlights on.

I see the headlights, I see the deer, I hear the loud bang, I feel the jolt, I hear my father's anguished sob. A breathless shock engulfs me, even now. The deer's face materializes before me, vividly illuminated by the starkness of our headlights. Do I imagine its terror, or am I recalling my own panic? I'm not sure. But I am certain about my father's cry. It is a deep, guttural gasp of pain, unleashed from somewhere deep within him. It lasts only a second. But it will echo in my mind forever, like the distant sound of a wolf's howl.

I have never discussed this moment with my father. There are certain things I know are better left unsaid. Things I don't question, or ask about. I don't press him for details about his life in the work camps in Germany and France. A few times in my life, mostly when I was still quite young, he opened up briefly about his childhood. He told me he was one of the boys who smuggled food over the walls of the Warsaw Ghetto. He told me that someone sent him to a prison when he was eleven years old to keep him safe, and he learned to speak Czech from a fellow prisoner there. Today my father speaks seven languages. English was his last. Polish, his first, he refuses to speak.

My father told me he was on the last train out of the Warsaw Ghetto before the uprising. He was reunited with his father in a camp in Germany, and eventually with his mother and three sisters at a work camp in France. My grandfather, who died before I was born, bribed the security guards at the camp to keep moving his family lower down the list of the Jews being sent by train to Auschwitz. Finally their names were at the top of the list. On the day they were scheduled to board the train, the French camp was liberated. His brother-in-law died in Auschwitz, but my father was free.

I am not sure about these things. They are what my father

told me, or what I think he told me. I cannot ask him. He rarely speaks about the past.

I see the headlights, I see the deer, I hear the loud bang, I feel the jolt, I hear my father's anguished sob. But what did my father see or do that night? I don't think there was time to swerve. We were driving on a peaceful country road, with no other cars in sight. All was tranquil. Perhaps the radio was playing. Perhaps my father was saying something to me. I imagine he was enjoying being at the wheel of his little Czechoslovakian car. But then the deer was there, in the windshield. I am sure my father slammed on the brakes. I am sure it was too late.

I was shaken to the core; the car was banged up. The deer, this exquisite, gentle creature, was dead. And my father cried.

My memory of the deer is brief, fleeting. Its back was light brown, like thick sea sand, damp from a summer rain. I don't remember antlers; it must have been a doe. But the rest could be my own creation from fractured memory: the quick turn of her head toward the car, the terrified look in her eyes, the flash of white at the bottom of her tail. Blood on the road. Did I just add the blood on the road?

Was she young, I wonder? Was she alone, or following in the path of another deer that had crossed just before her? Was a fawn waiting in the shadows among the trees? Had she lived a good life, was she happy, did she feel fear, did she know that death had come? Or was it quick, just a moment, and then over?

The deer could have crossed a minute before, or a minute after. She could have ducked back into the trees at the sound of our little Czechoslovakian car approaching on the road.

And then I know I must let it go, before it crushes me.

# CHAPTER ONE

# No One Watches the Old Lady Dance

The sun warms my legs as they lie on the edge of a white plastic lawn chair. I have always felt critical when I look at my legs, at least since the age of fourteen. They are, after all, too large, too muscular, marked in places with small, white keloid scars. I remind myself that these legs are strong; in a few weeks they will have carried me through forty years. Just this week they hiked to the summit of Mount Sanitas, a quarter mile from the house I rent in Boulder, Colorado. Yet I wrestle with ambivalence about my hips, and soon I look away. My body and me, approaching middle age, not speaking.

A chill in the air forecasts fall. I cross my arms, trying to snuggle more tightly into my old, worn-out sweatshirt. The flower garden is tangled and ragged, retreating from its summer glory. A few red and white roses remain. They bask in the sunshine among the remnants of what was once a chorus of colors transformed daily by blooms. My arms cramp up. I reach above my head, grasp one hand in the other, and stretch, feeling my shoulders pop.

Above my head, magpies quarrel with two squirrels in a canopy of leaves. The grass is lush now, neatly mowed, a green gift of the September rains that have washed away the parched, brown summer. Cool air trickles into my lungs. I attempt a deep breath, but my chest feels shallow. Three years ago when I moved to Colorado, I was thirty-six and alone. I'd traveled from New York to Boston, then to England, New York again, Israel, and back to New York. Wherever I landed, my life started, stopped, revved up again, sputtered. I could never get comfortable. Things kept falling apart.

I had hoped that Boulder, on the edge of the mountains and inviting to thirty-somethings without wedding rings, would become my home. This hope persisted for a couple of years. I've loved living among the skiers and the bike paths, but now I'm restless again. I'm still alone, and soon I'll be forty. Does the tightness in my chest reflect a sense of foreboding? It could be simpler than that—caused only by the smoke and haze hanging in the sky after a summer of blazing wildfires.

I've been told that life is less painful if you stay in the present, dismiss the past, and avoid thoughts of the future. Be here, now. So I try to stay here, with my breath and the smoke and the sky and the sun on my skin. But memories beat their fists at my door and beckon through the windows with crooked fingers. I am tempted and give in; my mind slips out.

I see an eleven-year-old girl. A boy is teasing her, calling her "button chest." She is embarrassed by the changes in her body. She wants to run fast like the boys. Her mother is at home doing laundry, depressed. The girl doesn't want to end up like her mother. She doesn't like dolls; she wants to be strong. Her body is betraying her.

Now the girl is thirteen. They didn't let her join the Little League team; they won't let her play soccer at school. She joins the gymnastics team. She has dark eyes, pigtails, and a clear-skinned face. She dances on the mat, dips down and stretches, moves in time with the recorded music. She reaches toward the audience, turns and stands straight, pauses for a moment at the corner of the mat. She raises herself on her toes as the music speeds up. Then she runs, turns and twists, tumbles in the air, and lands standing on the mat, arms up. Her chin lifts, and she flashes a smile. The audience applauds. The judges' pencils move quickly across clipboards.

Older selves replace the thirteen-year-old girl. They appear and recede at a distance. A high school girl in a peasant costume sings "Matchmaker" on an auditorium stage. She is told her performance was affecting, but the next day she pulls on her gymnastics leotard and stares at her body in the mirror. She is embarrassed by the size of her hips. At the end of the day she writes in her diary, listing every calorie she put in her mouth. The boys eye the cheerleaders who have slim, perfect legs, wear lipgloss, and blow-dry their hair. She knows that is what it means to be pretty, and she also knows she is not that. She wants the boys to like her, but not for the things that she wishes she could make disappear.

A college student with long, unkempt hair, in patched blue jeans and a Grateful Dead t-shirt sits alone at the edge of a pond near her dorm. During summer break, her boyfriend visits. He lifts her shirt and glances at her backside. "Not bad," he says. She is glad that she has not gained weight.

A woman in Boston, twenty-seven now, says a tearful good-bye to a man who is leaving. She should not bother to cry. She won't see him again for five years, and when she does she will no longer care. But I can't tell her this; she stops eating and drops to 103 pounds. She thinks her reflection in the mirror finally looks good, but her friends at work ask if she is sick. She leaves. She boards a plane for Israel, where she lives in the desert and takes Hebrew classes. She starts eating again and begins to gain weight, and berates herself for starting to look heavy.

She hikes through the desert and swims in the Dead Sea. She sings "On My Own" from *Les Misérables* at a small coffee-house, accompanied by a pianist. The people at the tables clap their hands. She has given another great performance.

I am back in the garden, watching one of the squirrels make his way down a tree toward the roses. Upside down, he clings to the bark and stops to lift his head, assessing any danger I might present. "I won't bother you," I tell him. The squirrel understands and continues his descent. I glance at a nearby Tupperware dish to be sure there is water inside. I started leaving water for the squirrels after one of them followed me around one morning in the middle of the scorching summer. I was watering the flowers, and he drank from the end of the hose.

How I crave a sip of my own gentleness.

Friends have been relentless in their crusade to convince me that forty is not old. It's a beginning, they explain, not an end. "Remember," one said, "on your birthday you are just one day older." Still, I sense that I am running out of time.

My mind slips away again. The woman, twenty-nine, is back in the States. She sits in a doctor's office. She is shaking, her mother beside her. Now she is wheeled into an operating room. She panics, and the nurses sedate her. A hot, white light hangs above her head. She sees masked faces. Hands pat her arms gently in an attempt to offer comfort. Voices grow softer, more distant. Tears slide down her cheeks. She has a tumor. They will fix it, but she will never have children.

Her body has betrayed her.

Back in the garden, I focus fiercely on the red and white roses. They blur as tears sting my eyes. It occurs to me that my body and I have been estranged for a decade. I have been banished from the only shelter I ever occupied. But did my body betray me? Or did a childhood battle become a full-blown war?

My mind drifts back a few days. I am taking a dance class in a dimly lit exercise studio. Dirt from the wood floor grinds into my feet. Hot spots burn my toes where blisters are forming. Still, I dance, twist and turn with three other women in the class. The teacher is slim and young, with a blond ponytail and a small tattoo of a rose on her right shoulder. She wears black stretch pants and a tiny tank top. Noticing the top, I feel ashamed and embarrassed. Beneath the embarrassment is anger I stuff down. My chest is too large for tiny tank tops, and I must be careful to wear shirts that hide scars. I glance into the mirror and wait for the voice that I know will soon enter my head. It happens when my right arm moves up. My shoulders and arms are too thick, it says. My legs are too large. I glance at the legs of the woman beside me. She is thin and pretty and sleek, and I wish that I looked like her.

In the garden, I stare at my hands. They are red, the skin dry. I lift them and hold them up to the sky.

I am here, yet somewhere else, not now, someday. The garden is knotty and tangled and old, but I understand that it was once beautiful. In fact, it is still beautiful. I see disarray but also past glory, and have affection for them both. I hear music and feel my body dancing. My hair is long and gray, and it tickles the bare skin on my shoulders. When my arms move to the side, there is a twinge of pain. Still, I move with the music. My legs bend, and my hips begin to sway. I smile and turn my face to the sun, then lower my arms and hug my chest. I take a deep breath. I am home.

No one watches the old lady dance, just a cat who sits on the fence. Or maybe the cat is watching the magpies. They are quarreling with the squirrels in the leaves above my head, on a cool September day in Boulder, Colorado, three weeks before my fortieth birthday.

# CHAPTER TWO

# The Diversion

I remember that cold Colorado night like one might remember a lost hope. It was a pipe dream colored in blue, green, and orange red, a Rocky Mountain landscape sprinkled with snow. The dark sky stretched out forever, stars glinted, and the table-flat plains flew out into the horizon.

We'd seen *Crouching Tiger, Hidden Dragon*, and our heads were filled with images of noble warriors from ancient times, heroes who could fly, pastel fabrics flowing in the wind, eroticism, forbidden love. Despite or maybe because of the cold, venturing out meant defiance; it was our nod to youth. We walked to the edge of town, our feet warm in worn winter boots. We made our way up a winding footpath toward towering red rocks silhouetted against the night sky, eerie like ghosts or Easter Island faces. When we had climbed high enough, we sat on the cold ground between the rocks, huddled close to each other, protected against the bursts of wind that swirled through the mountains.

We were perched on the edge, alone.

You put your arm around me and held me close, and we sat in silence, staring out over the glimmering lights of the town. From such a height, the buildings looked like sand castles. We were peaceful, on the edge of something solid but one step away from nothingness, our cheeks glowing red with cold and emotion.

You spoke, asking the question of yourself more than me. "Why don't we do this every night?"

*Because you have a girlfriend, I thought. And I am not her.*

CHAPTER THREE

# Walden, Revisited

*"Keep the time, observe the hours of the universe, not of the cars."*
— Henry David Thoreau

A cool, fall breeze skims over Walden Pond, kicking up small waves that ripple across the water. I sit cross-legged on the cold, hard ground littered with pebbles and acorns. Behind me, a steep hillside borders Route 126, a paved road that winds through Lincoln, passes Walden Pond, and heads toward Concord center. I have traveled that road many times. But today I want to slow down, sit still, check in.

The trees surrounding the pond hint at fall. Flashes of yellow and orange peek through the canopy of green. The woods smell of earth, pine, and decaying leaves. Behind my laptop, which I set on top of a low stone wall, the sixty-one-acre pond stretches toward the opposite shore. The nearby beach has been underwater since spring, when heavy rains flooded much of Massachusetts. A sliver of dry sand remains. For months I believed that the flooding would subside, and Walden Pond would return to the boundaries I've always known. But it occurs to me now that this might never happen. The shape of the pond might be forever changed.

It is incongruous that I brought a laptop to Walden Pond,

one of America's most enduring symbols of nature. In the past, I stuffed a notebook and pen into a backpack and wandered to a lonely rock at the edge of the water. I still do that sometimes. But for years I gripped pens too tightly in my hand out of eagerness to get my thoughts down on paper. Now I find it painful to write that way. I'm a fast typist, so my thoughts flow freely from mind to computer, but I wonder if the writing is the same. I suspect something has been lost in the disconnection between hand, pen, and ink, between ideas and physical pages I could touch. I sense that my connection to the land and pond has also slipped, like the trees whose roots are now suffocating underwater. Perhaps this is the reason I am here today. This disconnection is more than a shame. It is a loss too important to ignore, a threat to the very essence of how I want to live my life.

Glancing up at the sky, I think of Colorado, where I lived for four years. Out West the sky stretched so far and wide it reminded me daily of my irrelevance. There was comfort in that. In Boston I am lucky if I glimpse the sky between rows of aging rooftops and sagging telephone wires. It is a backdrop that encourages a loss of perspective and a tendency to give weight to perceived misfortunes. I spend my days fighting setbacks that exist only in my mind. The sky sets me straight. I miss it.

I sit for a while and look at the pond, write, and then look up again. Two women in warm coats and sturdy boots approach. They are headed toward the trail that circles the pond. It picks up to my left at the end of the wall, just past a public boat ramp. As the women step behind me, one of them glances casually at my laptop. "Can you get Wi-Fi at Walden Pond?" she asks.

The question surprises me. I look at her and smile. "I don't know; I haven't tried," I reply.

The woman nods and walks on. A chipmunk dashes behind a nearby tree.

Wi-Fi at Walden Pond. The thought triggers a wave of despair. But the pond, stretched before me, is more than a hundred feet deep. It swallows my sadness.

Walden Pond, surrounded by woods and hiking trails, is the central attraction of a modern state park. The park is quiet on this chilly October afternoon; most people are at work or at school. In the summer, swimmers flock to the nearby boathouse, opening and slamming its rickety screen doors. But today the boathouse is locked, and its windows are shuttered. Only one door to a storage area stands open.

Black-capped chickadees flit among the trees as waves lap gently against the shore. The muffled drone of car engines is a constant reminder, however, that a major roadway passes the pond to the north, hidden by a narrow stand of trees. Walden Pond, although peaceful and bucolic on a quiet day, is just a half hour's drive from downtown Boston. Thankfully, no skyscrapers are visible from here. When I look up, I see branches swaying gently in the breeze. The bright sunlight, hidden periodically by gray clouds, bounces in fragments off the water.

Having jogged the trail around the pond many times, I can picture every turn, dip, and hill. Water licks at the tree roots near a small, secondary beach on the eastern shore of the pond. This summer that beach is also flooded, and swimmers deposited their portable chairs and canvas bags in the woods. Farther down the trail, stairs fashioned from rocks descend to the edge of the water. About halfway around, not far from the spot where Thoreau's cabin once stood, you can view the boathouse from a distance, across the full length of the pond. If you continue counterclockwise, a railway abruptly appears at the top of the steep slope. A train rumbles by on a regular schedule, carrying commuters to and from Boston. I always imagined the people inside wearing tailored suits and reading the *Wall Street Journal,* and wondered if any of them looked up to see the pond.

I was always so glad not to be on that train.

A bird with a long neck floats on the surface of the pond and dips its head into the water. In an instant, the bird disappears. A few seconds later it resurfaces for air. *Is it a cormorant?* I wonder. I'm not sure. I watch it disappear again and then re-appear.

A red canoe floats by, thirty feet from the shore. The man and woman it carries dip their paddles and pull them gently through the water. Their lightweight jackets flap steadily in the breeze. The canoe slides away, leaving a triangular wake. After a few moments the ripples fade away.

Two park rangers rake pine needles from the water as they work their way along the edge of the beach. They leave the needles in piles near the pond and carry their rakes toward the boathouse. I think, *Just a little more wind, and the water will pull those needles right back in.*

When I jogged around the pond every morning, I would arrive about six o'clock. Few people could be found in the park at that hour: a photographer steadying a camera on a tripod perhaps, or an elderly hiker leaning on a walking stick. Some-times I passed a lone fisherman poised at the water's edge with a rod and reel. I understood the fisherman's wish to enjoy the quiet morning, but never his desire to catch a fish.

I am beginning to understand why I came here today. I needed to escape the cluttered struggles of everyday life, the battles born of a false sense of consequence. I spend so much time waving a sword in the air; I am exhausted and want to lay my weapon down. Like Don Quixote, I have been tilting at windmills.

The sun emerges from behind a gray cloud, brightening, for a moment, the color among the leaves. The pond is trans-formed from brooding to cheerful. An elderly woman sits on the stone wall near the boathouse, wearing an ankle-length coat and a black hat. She eats a sandwich or an apple (I can't tell from this distance), and stares thoughtfully at the water.

My face and hands are cold now, and my fingers feel stiff as they seek the letters on the keyboard. I have been sitting beside the pond for an hour and soon will have to stop writing.

Suddenly I remember the question that woman asked as she walked past me earlier. I move my cursor to the bottom of the screen and click on the words: *Connect to a Network*.

A message flashes quickly across the screen. "Windows cannot find any networks."

I breathe a sigh of relief. The sky still stands guard over the chickadees and the chipmunks, over the trees and the wind, over Walden Pond and me. All I need to stay connected is here.

# CHAPTER FOUR

## Tulips

Last fall I planted tulips in a patch of dirt behind the house I share with my new husband. They started poking through the soil this week. I didn't realize the shoots would emerge so early. It is only mid-April, and cold wind still whistles through the backyard at night, shaking the bare tree branches. The sky remains interminably gray. When I step outside, pull on a fleece jacket, and look up at the sky, I rarely see stars.

I developed an interest in gardening two years ago, when Jean-Paul and I moved into our old, run-down house in a working-class suburb of Boston. Jean-Paul's mother purchased the house as an investment and then became ill, so we bought the place from her. It was the only way we could afford to own our own home. Built in 1837, the house has an ancient, patched stone foundation. The thick support beams in the basement resemble trees, and the crooked wooden floors creak underfoot. I am certain the house was once lovely and new, but structurally it no longer is what it was. If I had to choose one word to describe it, I'd call the house "broken."

When the house became ours, I was determined to spruce it up. With a limited budget, we couldn't do much to fix the interior, so I cast around for ways to cheer up the property. We enclosed the backyard in a new white fence, but couldn't afford to do any serious landscaping, or to remove what was left of an old garage near the back, a cracked cement floor and the first three rows of gray cinder block walls. Sometimes I wonder, as I wrestle our lawnmower over the weeds that grow through the cracks in that floor, what the garage might have looked like when it was new, and whole, and had a purpose for being here.

Planting flowers was one thing I could do. I knew nothing about gardening but hoped I could learn. How difficult, I thought, could it be? Living things tend to thrive in my care. So I strode through the garden center at a nearby Home Depot as Jean-Paul pushed a large cart behind me. We piled bags of red mulch into the cart, and I added trays of colorful marigolds and two small trowels for digging.

The next day we pulled on jeans, t-shirts, and gardening gloves, and dug trenches near the front door and in back of the house, next to the old wooden deck. The marigolds caused an immediate effect—suddenly, there was color everywhere. I wandered around the house, admiring our handiwork; and over the days and weeks that followed I weeded, watered, and watched the flowers bloom and spread as the beds thickened throughout July and into August.

Then the cold air of fall blew in. My marigolds withered, turned brown, and died. The sight of their dried leaves and stems was depressing. To cheer me up, my friend Kathy, an expert gardener, suggested that I plant tulip bulbs. They would sleep all winter under the ground, she explained, and then break through the dirt and bloom in the spring. Tulips don't just die and disappear; they come back year after year. It sounded too good to be true.

I drove back to Home Depot and grabbed a few bags of tulip bulbs off the shelves. Once home I hurried to the backyard with the bags, a trowel, and my dirt-stained gardening gloves. I laid everything out on the ground and read the planting instructions on the sides of the bags. I started digging holes in two separate areas near the deck and placed the bulbs a few inches apart in the holes. Then I covered them with the displaced dirt and watered the whole area with the garden hose.

When the job was finished, I surveyed the patches of sloppy wet dirt, envisioning what would be my new gardens next spring. The hardest part would be waiting all winter to see if the tulips would grow.

Fall came and went. The ground cooled and hardened, and the leaves of the maple, cherry, and crabapple trees turned orange, red, and brown. Eventually they fell off the branches. We raked the leaves and stuffed them into lawn bags for the town to cart away. Everything froze. December arrived and snow began to fall, and neighbors decorated their houses with holiday lights. The new year came, followed by a long, dark January and a frigid February. Snow fell, melted, then fell again. February turned into March. Through it all, the ground was solid, frozen, and silent.

When April arrived, I finally allowed myself to hope for the end of winter. Kathy called and suggested I check to see if my tulips were pushing up through the ground. Excited, I hung up the phone, hurried out to the yard, and crouched down to examine the earth, forgetting to throw something warm over my sweatshirt. I shivered in the cold and hugged my arms against my chest. Scanning the area I had planted in the fall, I searched for any evidence of new life. Then I saw them—tiny green leaves peeking up through the dirt.

I reached out a hand and brushed away some old, dried leaves that had settled in the dirt. I stared at the tulip shoots for a very long time. And then, without warning, I started to cry.

By the time Dr. Kleiner called me into his office, I had been struggling with health issues for nearly a year and had been through two other doctors. I was just twenty-nine when fibroid tumors, assumed to be benign, were discovered in my abdomen. The first doctor, a gynecologist in Westchester

County, New York, believed I could live with the fibroids. She almost rolled her eyes when I returned several months later and insisted that something was very wrong. But she changed her tune after my blood tests came back and revealed extreme anemia. By the time I was rushed into my first surgery, a myomectomy that would remove the growing fibroids but keep the uterus intact, I needed two blood transfusions.

I should have been all right after that. I was weak and in pain, but on the road to recovery, my hope to have children in the future preserved. But unexpectedly, the pathology lab flagged one of the tumors. Something about the cells looked suspicious.

I had been told that fibroid tumors are benign more than 99 percent of the time. My doctor and the surgeon who had performed the myomectomy considered this development very odd. Without informing either me or my parents, they sent the slides with my tissue samples to five different pathologists. Finally the slides landed in a lab at Massachusetts General Hospital, where the world's foremost expert on this type of tumor declared a diagnosis: "a smooth muscle tumor of unknown malignant potential."

Three months had passed since the myomectomy. I had progressed from initially being able to move only gingerly to walking for five minutes at a time on the treadmill, then ten. I was slowly rebuilding my life. This new diagnosis confused me and my parents, who had opened their house to me, and Aaron, the man I had been dating since we had met in Israel a year before my health problems started. What did "unknown malignant potential" mean? Did I have cancer?

No one could say for certain if I did have cancer or if this news meant, in fact, that I soon would. So I made an appointment with Dr. Kleiner, a leading gynecological surgeon at Montefiore Hospital in New York City. After reviewing my case, he called a group of specialists together to discuss treatment options. One of the major concerns was how to preserve a young, unmarried woman's ability to have children.

Now Dr. Kleiner was ready to share the doctors' opinions. My parents accompanied me to his office. As soon I walked into the room and sat down in a chair near his desk, I could tell from the somber look on his face that the news would not be good. His manner was fatherly; in fact, he was a Holocaust survivor from Poland like my own father. The two men spoke to each other in Polish, a language that I don't understand and that my father usually refuses to speak. Then Dr. Kleiner sat down in a chair facing mine and leaned toward me. He looked me steadily in the eyes and explained the situation as gently as he could. The doctors could not agree about whether or not I already had cancer or about my chances of developing cancer if I did not have a hysterectomy. One specialist was convinced that I was all right and thought my chance of developing cancer with no surgery was as small as 5 percent. Another said the chance was as high as 25 percent. I had a choice about whether or not to have the surgery, Dr. Kleiner explained. But if I didn't, he wanted me to understand that I would have to have an X-ray and ultrasound every three months for the rest of my life so they could watch for signs of disease. And by the time the evidence presented itself—by the time they found cancer—it would probably be too late to save my life.

"If you were my daughter," Dr. Kleiner said to me, "I would tell you to get that thing out of there right now."

That thing was my uterus, something that once, what seemed like a long time ago, had been a private part of my body. Before I got sick I had never discussed my body with anyone, not even my mother. I had kissed only two boys before age sixteen, and one of those was during a game of spin the bottle. I had been painfully shy with the few men I dated in college and in my twenties. But since I'd gotten sick, my privacy had been wrenched away from me. My body had been laid out under glaring hot lights for the entire world to see. I had been touched, roughly and mechanically, by the hands of doctors, nurses, and medical technicians, all strangers. They had examined me and prodded my most private parts in ways that filled me with shame and embarrassment. What I didn't recognize for many months was that the shame was obscuring a deepening rage. I began having nightmares and anxiety attacks, and was put on antianxiety medication. All medical tests caused me to shake and panic. I was advised to listen to music through headphones during tests, to avoid looking at the technologists' faces so I wouldn't read anything into their worried frowns. I was supposed to treat myself to something special after every appointment, even if it was just an ice cream. Meanwhile, my ultrasound films and tissue samples were being passed around the hospital, the city, the country.

It was not common for doctors to recommend a hysterectomy to a childless woman of my age. Before the appointment, I had sought comfort in any information I could find about my condition and a possible hysterectomy. Once, I picked up a feminist medical book titled *Our Body, Our Selves*, which had been written, supposedly, to help empower women. The book decried hysterectomies and adoption as misogynistic. Now, as Dr. Kleiner spoke to me, I felt the eyes of the women who'd written that book fixed on me in hot disapproval. In the end, they were laying as much claim to my body as the doctors. Everyone wanted a piece of me.

By the time Dr. Kleiner stopped speaking, I was staring straight at the floor. Something tasted bitter at the back of my mouth. My throat constricted. I told myself silently that the doctors had done all they could. I had tried to get through this thing whole. I had prayed to God every night that they would not have to cut me open again. It just wasn't meant to be.

Dr. Kleiner and I both knew that one thing he had told me wasn't true. I did not have a choice. I had just turned thirty; I could not spend whatever time I had left waiting for cancer and death. As for having a child, for all anyone knew, I couldn't have one by now anyway.

My hands, white in their own tight grip, blurred as tears dripped off my face, onto my shoes and the floor. I nodded, giving my consent.

Aaron stood by me through the hysterectomy. We got married two years later, but I was still too damaged to make a marriage work. Within two years we filed for divorce, as amicably as two people can. He remarried a year later when his girlfriend became pregnant.

Jean-Paul and I met at forty-one, and married at forty-four. We're forty-five now. We have talked about adoption, but the timing has never seemed right. My guess is it never will.

I sometimes picture my little girl in my mind (for some reason she has always been a little girl). I imagine her with brown eyes and dark curly hair, like mine, or with pale eyes like my father's and Jean-Paul's. She's lively and precocious, sensitive and full of laughter. She hugs goats and kisses kittens and runs in circles in the yard, her arms flung up in the air. She loves chocolate and gets it all over her face. She is talented at music like Jean-Paul, and she sings like an angel. She is full of life.

But I will never know her. So I fuss over Jean-Paul, and I fuss over our cats. The truth is, I like to love things.

Every day since Kathy called, I go outside to look at my tulips. I kneel in the dirt and reach toward them, gently feel their soft, green leaves between my fingers. Every time I visit they are a little bigger. Their leaves are wider, spreading up and out toward the sky. The tulips are undisturbed by the rain that comes and goes, or by the cold breeze that still picks up at night.

As April advances, the sun appears more often in the

sky. The temperature has climbed out of the forties and into the fifties. It will hit sixty soon. When I sit outside, I hear neighborhood children behind our back fence, enjoying the sunshine in nearby yards. They laugh, bounce basketballs in their driveways, call out to each other. Sometimes their music blares from car radios or boom boxes. They stand nearby while their parents cook hamburgers and hot dogs on outdoor grills. I smell the propane and barbecue sauce, and watch the pale-gray smoke as it rises into the twilight.

I am waiting now for my tulips to flower. If I remember the pictures on the bags correctly, some will be red, some yellow, some orange, some pink. It is possible there will be other colors too.

It doesn't matter, when I am with my flowers, if the rest of the yard is beautiful. It doesn't matter if the inside of the house still needs work. It doesn't even matter if I will ever feel truly whole. The tulips don't care about all that. They just need me to water them and watch them grow. Just by existing, they give me a kind of uncomplicated delight. It is a precious thing to still be here, to still be able to feel that. So I let it in, and stay with it for as long as I can.

# CHAPTER FIVE

# Up to Nothing

Jean-Paul sits in our Subaru Outback, staring hard through the rain-drenched windshield. He is driving us north from Boston to New Hampshire. Last night we packed two large duffels with the usual gear: Camelbacks, Gore-Tex boots, windbreakers, energy bars. Our plan for the weekend has been set for months. Today we will explore the Sunapee region. It's been a long time since I've been there, but I've mapped out the trip in my head. First we'll check in at the Burkehaven Inn and unload our clothes and gear. After exploring the town and visiting Lake Sunapee, we'll have dinner at a lakeside restaurant that has a bar on the deck. Tomorrow we'll hike up to Mount Sunapee's summit. According to an Internet site that I found, there is a trail through the woods near the ski slopes. The views are spectacular at the top. After we've absorbed all that, we can hike back down, maybe sip a cold beer in a lodge at the base.

I want to enjoy these images of the weekend ahead, but I keep thinking about leaving my mother-in-law. Michael, Jean-Paul's uncle, is visiting from San Antonio, so Judith will not be alone. Still, she did all she could to make this difficult. Her eyes turned red and filled with tears when my husband told her we'd be gone for a few days. She slumped in her wheelchair with her shoulders forward and her head hanging down.

Then she said in a voice both childlike and angry, "What if I run out of medicine?"

"Michael is here," Jean-Paul reminded her.

"I don't want to ask Michael to do things," she spat.

*But you don't mind asking us to do everything*, I thought, feeling bitchy.

"I'll be happy to get you your medicine, Judy," Michael said, trying to soothe her. Jean-Paul's uncle is in his midseventies, retired from the Air Force, tall and slim. He works out every day. For a weekend he can handle his sister's needs. Still, she put her head in her hands and sobbed, as if her son had announced he was abandoning her for good.

Judith was an unusual person before all this happened: statuesque and slim, quirky and self-centered, temperamental and creative, subtly controlling. Sometimes, during the two years I've known her, she surprised me with unexpected kindnesses—thoughtful gifts on holidays, toys for our cats.

I think back to the day we learned Judith had brain cancer. She was scheduled to have a benign growth removed from the lining around her brain. Just a few days before the operation, the neurosurgeon sat in a chair in her hospital room and looked her straight in the eye, "You do not have cancer," he told her. "You won't die from this."

He was wrong.

He discovered his mistake in the operating room. Realizing the tumor was inside the brain, he performed a biopsy and closed up her skull. Jean-Paul and I, married just three months at the time, had been driving around Cambridge. We were waiting for news that the surgery was over, thinking things were going according to plan. Judith was wheeled into the ICU; a nurse called to beckon us back to the hospital. Something in the tone of her voice made us nervous. When we walked into the waiting room, the surgeon motioned for us to join him in a tiny side office. We sat on two wooden chairs pulled up to a desk, and he told us what had happened. He shook his head. If the tumor was what he suspected, a glioblastoma, Judith had maybe eighteen months to live. Tests on the tissue would take a few days. Jean-Paul and I were silent at first, in shock. We asked a few questions. I stepped outside the office to let Jean-Paul handle details. Then I leaned my back against a wall and cried.

I visited Judith every day those first months. She was, after all, my new mother-in-law. I cleaned her small, empty house and picked up her mail. I fed, and then adopted, her cats. She was moved from the ICU to a regular room before being admitted to a rehabilitation facility. Bleeding after the biopsy caused swelling in her brain and paralysis on the left side. Judith spent months recovering what movement she could for whatever time she had left.

The social workers at Park Avenue Rehab told us to expect certain emotional stages: denial, anger, bargaining, depression, acceptance. Judith went from shock to denial and coupled that with rage, and has stayed there for more than a year. She refuses to believe the doctor's prognosis. She has spent forty thousand dollars on home renovations, ignoring the reality of the time she has left. She demanded her staircase be rebuilt three times before finally admitting she would never walk up the stairs. That made her so angry she threatened to sue the contractor. She can't get in or out of her house without help yet insists on living alone. She can't shop for herself or count her own pills. She relies on us for all her errands. "I hope this happens to you someday!" she screams at her only child, Jean-Paul.

I know that Judith is not who she was; but the truth is, neither am I. The person I was would feel guilty, even sad, leaving a sick person behind. I don't feel those things. I feel numb, I feel tired. I even feel angry. All I want is to get out of Boston.

The rain started before dawn this morning. It hammered on the roof of our house as we pulled ourselves out of bed, dressed in warmer clothes than we had thought we would need, and sprinted in and out of the house to load the car. By the time we slid into the front seats we were soaked; our faces were cold and dripping with rain. The downpour has continued throughout the drive, but we are on an adventure and thrilled to be getting away.

We exit the highway after two hours and follow a small, winding road to the Burkehaven Inn. An online search led me here; the website depicted a charming hotel nestled in a valley, surrounded by woods. It was close to Sunapee's mountain and lake, and the white wood siding with red trim gave it the look of a classic Colonial inn.

As we pull into the driveway, I notice that the grounds have changed since the photos were taken. A tall house has been built just below the inn on what was once part of the spacious green lawn. The house almost blocks the view of Mount Sunapee, and it's not the only building nearby. Homes with paved driveways and fenced-in backyards line the streets near the inn. Apparently we'll be staying in the middle of a residential neighborhood.

The inn itself is what I expected, if a little small. It is L shaped and single level, with the exception of a second-floor addition above the angle in the L. We park in front of a sign that says Lobby and dash from the car to two glass doors, our heads bent against the still-pouring rain. The lobby is empty, but a note next to a telephone on a desk instructs visitors to call a number for assistance. Jean-Paul dials, and I hear a man on the other end of the line say he will be right with us.

A few minutes later a large red pickup pulls into the parking lot. A man about our age, in his forties, hops out of the truck and jogs across the parking lot through the rain. His face is half covered by a dark beard, and he wears a light jacket over a red flannel hunting shirt and blue jeans. He nods as he enters the lobby and heads for the desk, then scans a reservation book and asks, "DesPres?"

We both nod, and he jots down a note in the book before handing Jean-Paul a room key. "Looks like we're not too lucky with the rain," Jean-Paul says.

The innkeeper shakes his head and replies, "Well, what can you expect in May?"

Back in the car, I say to Jean-Paul, "I really thought it would be sunny and warm. I wanted to go to the lake and sit outside."

"I don't want to hear anything negative," he says. I understand the note of annoyance in his voice. I haven't been particularly cheerful lately. Judith's condition has worsened, and her tantrums and demands are affecting us both. I walk around our house like a cat with the hair on my back always up. Every time our phone rings I literally jump. Either it is Judith raging on the other end of the line or the hospital calling to report she has fallen, called 911, and been admitted again.

"She's insane and I can't take it!" I often yell in frustration.

"She's my mother" is all he can say.

My husband is a gentle soul, the child of divorced parents. His father died twenty years ago; it has been just Jean-Paul and his mom since then. For a year he has been more parent than child; but my guess, from the short time I knew Judith before, is that he's familiar with the role. I admire his ability to weather her outbursts and run her errands without losing control. But I do wonder lately if he'll break down at some point, or if he will simply explode.

Room #1 is the last room at the far end of the inn, near the driveway. We transfer our bags inside quickly. A king-size bed with a thick wooden headboard fills about a third of the room. A gas fireplace lends a cozy feel, along with a round breakfast table and two matching chairs, and an easy chair in front of an old TV set. There is a coffeepot and small refrigerator. I decide the room is nice, and Jean-Paul agrees, but we are anxious to get on with our day. We leave our things still packed in the room, dart back outside through the rain to the car, and head toward the center of town.

Sunapee is deserted. Wooden buildings seem to lean against the wind and rain as it washes the old empty streets. The lake is dark and restless. Restaurants are closed, doors locked, windows shuttered. Sailboats rock in the marina, firmly tethered to wooden docks, sails rolled up against the bad weather. There will be nothing for us to do in Sunapee.

We drive toward the next town and stop at an open tavern along a rural road. A noisy crowd fills most of the tables, but the hostess leads us to an empty wooden booth. We order sandwiches and local craft beer from a waiter who moves quickly between the tables, balancing a tray on his arm. I watch him, amazed at how waiters do that, and get caught up in the swirl of activity. Our sandwiches are made with thick, fresh-baked bread, and the French fries are hot and brown. The atmosphere is jovial among the local crowd. We smile at each other, and Jean-Paul tips generously. But when we step outside, the rain is still pelting down.

What now?

"The innkeeper said there's a cinema center half an hour away," I say, trying to keep the disappointment out of my voice. I didn't drive two hours or spend money on a hotel so we could waste the afternoon in a movie theater, but I can't think of anything else to do. Jean-Paul nods and pulls the car back onto the road, turning west toward the Vermont border. He remembers the innkeeper's directions, and we find the cinema center in a nondescript, cement strip mall in the middle of nowhere. The only film showing at that hour is *Iron Man*, starring Robert Downey Jr., a movie about a comic book hero who battles global terrorists. It's not my kind of movie, but we don't have much choice about what's happening to us today. We buy two tickets and go inside.

It's early-Sunday morning, and I'm sitting in front of the door of our room, hoping my halfhearted attempt to wipe down the white plastic chair on the wooden front porch made it dry. We discovered last night, after returning from the movie, that we are the only guests at the inn. Our Outback, lonely and wet in the rain, is parked not far from my chair. The only other vehicle in sight is the innkeeper's red pickup truck. I saw him pull out of the driveway of the house down below, drive up the road, swerve into the hotel parking lot, jump out of the front seat like he did yesterday, and disappear into the lobby. I hear the faint clattering of dishes as he prepares our breakfast.

It is seven o'clock, and Jean-Paul is asleep. Eternally restless, I wake up early; mornings are when I sit and think. I prepared hot coffee in the coffeepot and poured it into a Styrofoam cup. A quick sip tells me it has a bitter, chemical taste and is rapidly cooling off. I listen to the rain trickle off the roof, watch the drops form small pools in the gravel at the edge of the porch.

Jean-Paul joked yesterday that he would sit on this porch and enjoy the sunset and view if it killed him—even if he couldn't see the sun and there was no view. The rain had persisted, and the temperature by then had dropped down into the forties. He bundled up in layers, opened a bottle of red Zinfandel, and sat where I am sitting now. He sipped wine from a plastic cup and stared into the mist.

For four days now someone else has been by Judith's side. For these few brief days we have been almost free. But our freedom will be short-lived; it will end in just forty-eight hours. We'll go back to Boston, and Michael will return to Texas. Thinking about this, I take a deep breath and try to stay calm.

I hate the exhaustion, the resentment I feel. Judith refuses to pay for assistance when we know she easily could. She insists we handle everything and gets angry if we try to make time for ourselves. The lawn at our house is overgrown, tangled like an abandoned schoolyard. I've wrestled it all spring with a heavy, old push mower; but last week it was hot and I was tired. I asked Jean-Paul to do it for once. Judith accused him of lying when he told her he had to stay home. She resents my marriage and my house, tries to shove them into insignificance. Any effort to protest is considered self-centered. It occurs to me that I am trapped in the ultimate amplification of an age-old battle: mother-in-law vs. daughter-in-law. But my mother-in-law has a brain tumor. I am forced to forfeit.

Are these thoughts really crossing my mind? The woman is dying, and I am arguing with her. More than that, I am competing with her. I am ashamed that I feel this way. Lately, I don't even recognize myself.

Rivers of rain run through a cluster of white birch trees growing next to the porch. Tiny leaves bud on the branches, not yet open to the sky. The air, though damp, tastes fresh when I draw it into my lungs; I take slow, deep breaths, try to relax and get lost in the rhythm of the rain. It is cold, but my fleece jacket protects me from the chill. Thin cotton gloves shield my hands.

Every year when I was a child, I spent four weeks near this town, walking barefoot on sawdust paths, swimming in the cool, brown-tinted water of Baptist Pond. I dipped my hands in wet clay to make crooked pots, sang folk songs around late-night campfires, lay awake at night and stared at the stars through old window screens. Our camp was advertised as a "creative place for growing" and run like an antiwar peace rally. There was a lot of laughing and hugging and talk about friendship. We were encouraged to love one another like sisters and brothers. It was the freest, happiest time of my childhood. I climbed Mount Sunapee every summer back then; I wonder if that's why I am drawn to it now. I feel a need to put one foot in front of the other again and go up, up, up to the place we once found, and rescue myself from what feels so heavy and hard on the ground.

I need to know there is still beauty somewhere. I need to know I am still capable of finding it, feeling it. But when I planned this trip, I didn't count on the rain. I didn't count on the way the tips of my fingers are turning icy and numb inside my gloves right now. It feels as if fate always laughs in my face.

Just as the thought crosses my mind, something shifts. I hear it first, then see it. The hard pattering turns into pittering. The raindrops slow to a light drizzle. The ripples in the pools at the edge of the porch are less frequent and soon disappear. Drip by drip the rain stops. The fog begins to lift, and I look out across the valley. Mount Sunapee has emerged from the clouds, its slopes wide and dramatic, green and dark, finally visible through the mist.

Jean-Paul's face breaks into a smile, something I haven't seen in a while. The weather has cleared, and I see the sun reflected on his cheeks as he steps out onto the porch. "Time for breakfast?" he asks.

Our footsteps echo on the wooden front porch as we make our way toward the lobby. Glancing up as we enter through the glass doors, the innkeeper greets us warmly from the office nearby, where he is doing paperwork. After checking out the offerings, we pile English muffins, butter, and strawberry jam onto plates and sit down at the edge of a stone fireplace. The butter and jam taste sweet and sticky in my mouth, and the fresh-brewed coffee is smooth, piping hot. Colorful magazines advertise horseback riding, white-water rafting, antique stores, and other summer attractions. I notice an ad for the Craftsman's Fair, which will take place this August.

The air is still humid and cold when we step back outside, so we dress in warm layers and hiking boots. Water, cheese, crackers, and energy bars all go in the day pack. It's time to climb the mountain.

Mount Sunapee is the centerpiece of a state park just a few miles away from the Burkehaven Inn. There is a huge parking lot at the base, but today, like the lake, the mountain is desolate. The lodge and restaurants are closed; everything is silent and still. Now just three cars are in sight, dotted around the edge of the parking lot. They look like shapes in the corner of a cubist painting: lonely, abandoned, a little forgotten.

The base of the mountain, much wider and grander than we can grasp from our vantage point inside the car, rises out of the ground toward the sky. We roll down our windows and lean out for a better view, but can only see a few hundred feet up the slopes. "I wonder if there are rules about hiking the mountain during the off-season," I say, noticing no staff or park rangers in sight. Jean-Paul shrugs, uncertain.

We hear music coming from somewhere. Looking around, we realize the sound is pouring out of the windows of one of the restaurants, so we drive to the opposite side of the parking lot to investigate. Jean-Paul shuts off the engine and steps out of the car, walks over, and knocks on the door. No one responds. He returns to the car and settles back into the driver's seat. I look up again, notice that thick patches of wet, dirty snow still cling to the side of the mountain in spots, stubbornly resisting the onset of spring.

We sit silently for a couple of minutes, wondering what to do. Then a man emerges from behind one of the buildings. He is wearing a dark-blue rain jacket, jeans, and hiking boots, and is carrying a water bottle. Jean-Paul starts the car again and drives over to the man. "Hi there, do you know if it's all right to hike up the mountain?" Jean-Paul asks, leaning his head out the car window.

"I just did," the man responds with a smile. "No one ever bothers me. Do you know where the trail head is?" We shake our heads, and he points to an area behind an empty building that appears to house a closed ticket office or snack bar.

"It's back there; there's an orange traffic cone that marks the beginning."

We thank him, park the car, and unload our day pack. Jean-Paul agrees to carry it first. He swings the pack over his shoulders, and we start walking toward the trail.

The hiking trail on Mount Sunapee is not especially steep, technical, or difficult; but any uphill climb takes time, especially when conditions aren't perfect. We expect the hike to the summit to take two hours. Every inch of the trail is covered with exposed tree roots and thick piles of damp leaves. Navigating the path involves stepping over streams, circumventing fallen trees, and occasionally stubbing our toes on wet rocks. We slip, time and again, on dark, eroded soil. The effort requires concentration and persistence, so we plow forward largely in silence, pushing ourselves ever higher at a steady pace, breathing hard. Sometimes I find myself gasping for breath and have to stop for a minute. Now and then Jean-Paul pulls a water bottle out of the day pack so we can drink. I have a tendency to keep moving when I hike, to push and push and push to the top, because hiking is hard for me. I don't have a naturally strong lung capacity, and I'm afraid to admit it when something is hard for me. I don't want to disappoint other people or myself, be something less than I'm expected to be, so I hike and I hike and I hike and I hike. My companions have to stop me and say, "Breathe; take a drink."

Sweat pricks at our necks and dampens our backs. The air is fresh and clear, scented with pine, and Jean-Paul and I breathe it more deeply into our lungs. We can't see much along the trail; a moody light trickles through the early-spring leaves on either side of our path. Birds call to each other from the branches above our heads. With every step, my body and muscles feel warmer. My light rain slicker comes off first. I stuff it into the day pack. Farther up the trail, I pull off my fleece and tie the sleeves around my waist. I no longer feel the cold, not even on my face.

To be nearly alone on the mountain is eerie; toward the beginning of our trek, one lone hiker nodded a silent hello as he passed, walking quickly, on his way back down the trail. About a half hour later two athletic, gray-haired women strode by with their dogs trotting happily down the mountain beside them. Since then we have encountered no one and have hardly spoken to each other. We trudge on, put one foot in front of the other. Up, up, up.

Jean-Paul stops and points out a chipmunk he has noticed skirting through some leaves in the woods. I stop, too, and watch for a minute. We have been walking for nearly two hours now, and my muscles are tired. I am increasingly anxious for the end of the trail. Another hiker, the first one we've seen for ages, approaches on his way down the mountain.

"Are we close to the top?" Jean-Paul asks the man.

The hiker smiles, indicating with a quick nod the direction from which he came. "It's just there," he says.

A few yards ahead the trees recede. Suddenly we sense space all around us. We are at the summit, standing in front of a mountaintop ski lodge, surrounded by wide expanses of green. Breathing hard, I look around eagerly to see the view, but beyond the lodge and the lifts I see nothing. A thick, gray mist still hangs around the mountain. I can see that Jean-Paul has noticed the same thing.

My eyes meet his, and we burst out laughing. All that hard work for nothing! We've hiked to the top, and there is no view. We laugh and laugh. It is just too much. Maybe, in the end, there is no reward. Still, we jump, one by one, and land with our legs spread out and our arms stretching up to the sky.

None of this is what I dreamed it would be, but suddenly that is okay.

Jean-Paul is here. The mountain is here. I am still here. We celebrate as if we've reached the top of Everest.

# CHAPTER SIX

# *Survivors*

## I.

My father once threatened to beat Danny to a pulp, but at eighty-two he suffers from tremors. The tremors are getting worse. Last time I visited, his shoulders moved from side to side. His girth is still wide, and his legs are still muscular; but his arms have become thinner from lack of exercise. He used to lift a couch by himself. Now I lift his plate.

Diabetes has ravaged my father's body for four decades. His chest bears the scars of bypass surgery. But he has survived both, like the Warsaw Ghetto and the work camps in Germany and France. With Parkinson's, my father tells me that he will "harm himself" if he ever has to be "pushed." He means he'll kill himself if he has to be pushed in a wheelchair.

But I think he wants to live until God takes him.

## II.

My mother adopted a child because she wanted to save a life. My sister, born in Korea, stepped off the plane holding an escort's hand when she was five years old. Forty-three years later she learned that her birth father, an American soldier, lived with her mother for two years. He left when she was pregnant. Probably a military transfer.

My sister didn't make it through college; maybe it was too much to be torn from her adopted parents after first being torn from her birth mother. She moved back home, completed a secretarial course, and was working in the credit department of a local corporation when she started dating Danny. It wasn't until after they'd moved in together that she discovered the cocaine. He caught her flushing it down the toilet, and that's when he beat her up.

My sister showed up at my parents' door with two black eyes. They immediately pulled her into the house. Danny called. Danny cried. Danny said he was sorry. But my father threatened his life, and my sister stayed put. A security guard accompanied my parents to the apartment so they could retrieve my sister's things. Danny hid in a closet. My father pounded his fists on the closet door, but the security guard restrained him. Eventually my parents left.

My sister pressed charges, but all Danny got was probation. He went to prison a couple of years later for shooting a deer in a state park.

## III.

Fran is eighty-two, like my father. She is my mother-in-law's best friend. She remembers singing opera on the stage. She remembers teaching music and writing the dissertation that is credited to the man she loved. They never married, and he died long ago.

Fran doesn't remember falling in her home. She doesn't remember lying helpless on the floor or crying out when the cable guy knocked on the door. She doesn't understand how she ended up here, in a nursing home a mile from her house.

Fran's only living relative is a niece who lives eighteen hundred miles away. The niece will inherit Fran's estate. She flew in for a day and then left.

Fran lives in a plain rectangular room with two other residents. The room smells of ammonia, with a faint trace of urine. Curtains on rails separate the three beds. Fran stores clothes and a few books in a small, simple dresser next to her bed. She tells us that she can't sleep at night. When she does, she dreams about never going home.

"I don't want to die," she says while we sit at her bedside.

## IV.

The abandoned feral cat who lives in our backyard is almost pure white. She has two light-gray patches between her ears. Sometimes she sleeps in a small bed that I placed inside a doghouse that we found at the curb on garbage day. Sometimes she sleeps in the hollow of a dead tree, fifteen feet above the ground. I imagine she feels safer there. When she hears me filling the food dish in the morning, she climbs down, branch by branch. I stand near the tree and wait. When our eyes meet, it is like looking into a well filled with emeralds. The cat won't let me near her, so I retreat into the house and watch from the kitchen window until she jumps down and eats.

You say that I need to know more about God, but I think God needs to know more about me. What will I do to change the world?

Because God knows, it needs to be changed.

# CHAPTER SEVEN

# The Bird's Nest

Two thousand and eight Chinese Tai Chi masters move in unison on the TV screen that hangs on the waiting room wall. Close-ups reveal fierce dark eyes; but when the camera pulls back, the performers' bodies form massive, pulsing circles in the middle of the Bird's Nest, the Olympic stadium in Beijing. Unhappy to be back in a hospital waiting room, I lose myself in the pageantry. "It's incredible that two thousand human beings can create such perfect circles!" a commentator says. The Tai Chi masters, dressed in white uniforms, jump and twist, then land on the ground and freeze as one. Their movements are controlled, somehow weightless. Fabric billows around their taut bodies. I wonder how they know exactly where they are and where they fit, individually, into this colossal experience going on around them.

To the left of the TV, large red letters spell out EMERGENCY across two wide doors next to the registration desk. Jean-Paul and I rushed to the hospital after a nurse called to tell us his mother had fallen out of her wheelchair. It must be the hundredth time this has happened in the year and a half since she was diagnosed with a brain tumor. Judith refuses to consider moving into an assisted-living facility or paying for in-home care. She wheels herself around her small Cambridge house, a telephone clipped to the collar of her shirt. Each time she falls, she dials 9-1-1, and the local fire company sends an ambulance. If her door is locked when the EMTs arrive, they are forced to climb through a window. Usually, once they've put Judith back in her chair, she refuses to go to the hospital, so they are forced to leave her alone in the house. Sometimes we never find out about it. Apparently they overrode her angry protests tonight, because they transported her here.

A voice crackles over the PA system. "Mr. Stevens, Mr. Stevens."

I glance around the half-filled room and see a man I assume is Mr. Stevens. He stands up and walks toward the doors. I've been waiting at least an hour for my own name to be called, or for Jean-Paul to come back out to the waiting room and tell me what is going on. The doors open; Mr. Stevens walks through. The doors close again.

Tired and frustrated, I turn back to the television. I think about the Olympic motto: "Faster, higher, stronger." When I was young, this dream seemed possible, even for me, a small-town gymnast in upstate New York.

Now I watch the Tai Chi masters as they punch and kick the air, hear the force of their unifying "kiais," or yells. Tai Chi was one of the arts I practiced in my thirties when I studied martial arts. I remember part of the form we learned. At the beginning we held our hands in just the right way, then lifted our arms slowly with our elbows slightly bent. We arched our wrists, then reversed them so our palms led the hands back down as we breathed. In a slow, sweeping motion, with a turn at the waist, we switched direction and formed circles with our arms, one arm up, the other down. "Imagine you are cradling a large beach ball," our instructor used to say. The goal was connection, a sense of peace, the perfect circle.

Now the performers in the Bird's Nest encircle a group of schoolchildren. The children hug backpacks to their chests and smile as they watch the flow of activity around them. The commentator explains the symbolism involved. The circles represent the current generation as it protects the generation that follows.

I wonder if Judith ever protected Jean-Paul. She was emotionally fragile even before the brain tumor. A tall, blond beauty growing up in Missouri, she married her first love at twenty. They moved to Massachusetts with their son when he was six but divorced just a few years later. Judith stayed in Massachusetts but became anorexic and depressed, and suffered from bouts of rage and hysteria. When Jean-Paul was eleven, she packed her bags and threatened to move out. He had to block the doorway until she calmed down and agreed not to leave him alone. She was an unusually talented painter and sculptor, and settled into a career teaching high school art. For the next thirty years, she rarely dated, even though she remained slim and striking. She told me once that Jean-Paul's father, who died at forty-seven, would always be the love of her life.

The PA system intrudes again. "Maria Sanchez? Maria Sanchez?"

I try to ignore the interruption and turn my attention back to the Tai Chi masters. My throat has tightened over the thoughts of Judith, and I want to keep my feelings under control. She did not ask for this horrific illness. She would give anything for the last eighteen months to be a bad dream. Still, I feel my shoulders and neck start to stiffen, and I shift uncomfortably on the hard wooden chair. I have no desire to be here tonight. I don't even want to be myself in my life. I would rather be in China, in that stadium on TV. I would rather be a Tai Chi master. At the very least I would rather be home, watching the opening ceremonies in the comfort of my living room.

I notice a man in the waiting room. He is cradling a little girl in his arms. She has dark eyes and little black pigtails wrapped inside gray, shiny coils. They look like Mickey Mouse ears. The girl doesn't appear to be injured or ill, but she is crying. The man holds her and comforts her with gentle words. She notices the television mounted on the wall while tears stream down her face. The instant she sees the Tai Chi masters all dressed in white, moving in unison in perfect circles, the little girl stops crying. She just stares at them in wonder.

Judith told me once that she hated everything about her teaching career except, of course, her students. She was known to champion the underdogs, the kids who didn't fit in. At night she taught adult education classes. She set her own dreams aside for the future, when she would have a hefty retirement fund and a comfortable pension. When she finally retired with that pension in hand, her mortgage paid off and her son long grown, she started pursuing the things she wanted. She opened a business applying permanent cosmetics. She purchased closets full of shoes and new clothes. She bought a Porsche Boxster. Then she was diagnosed with a brain tumor.

The Tai Chi masters are leaving the stadium. A new group of performers pours into the arena and melts together to form a huge dove. A swarm of bodies, thousands of bodies, runs back and forth until the wings of the dove appear to be flapping up and down. The huge human bird is flying! I shake my head in disbelief. I cannot imagine how they do that. I think about the people of China, such a huge nation, putting on a show for the world. It strikes an emotional chord in me. They are trying to establish a new China, a new era for their country. Everything they demonstrate is beautiful, flowing, flying, as if nothing is more important than hope.

Recently, we learned that Judith's tumor is growing again; the doctors can't help anymore. The average patient with her type of tumor does not live long after diagnosis. Chemotherapy and radiation no longer work. Judith is furious, terrified. She blames everyone, including her son. She has insisted I want her to die.

When all this started, I felt grief and compassion; by now I am worn down and tired. Every day is painful and difficult, and we have had little time for ourselves. I am ashamed of my thoughts on this side of those doors, while my mother-in-law lies in a hospital bed.

A man just walked through the doors. He is talking to a woman who sits in a row of chairs right behind me. "We've decided to keep you here," he tells her. "We were planning to send you home; but we spoke to your insurance company, and we're going to keep you for the night."

I force my focus back to the television. How do the performers do it? Yet another group has entered the arena. They are dressed in glowing green costumes and have formed another massive circle. So many circles. They are hoisting themselves onto each other's shoulders, setting up for something big. The camera pulls back and then, yes, I see it! It is the Bird's Nest itself, the Olympic stadium! The stadium has been reconstructed, within itself, by thousands of human bodies. Now it is somehow flashing white and green. Ninety-one thousand people in the stands are enraptured. Each has been given a lantern to hold up. They are holding thousands of red lanterns with lights inside that flicker like cherry stars. The commentators are beside themselves, and so am I. The sight is so stunning that I can hardly breathe. One commentator says, "You might as well put away the trophy for opening ceremonies. This is it; no one will ever match it."

Everything on the screen is surreal, deeply and intensely beautiful. Everyone in the Bird's Nest is joyful and safe, oblivious to the world outside.

The PA buzzes to life again. "Kathy, please call the front desk. Kathy, front desk, please." I swat at the noise mentally as if it were a fly.

The performances at the opening ceremonies are coming to an end. The dancers turn and swirl, run off the floor. Announcers speak in French, then English, then Chinese. The parade of athletes begins. Men and women led by flag bearers march into the stadium. Some teams are dressed in suits, others in colorful folk costumes traditional to their cultures. I can't tell what order they are marching in; it is not alphabetical, at least not in English. The announcers' voices ring out over the loudspeakers and echo through the Bird's Nest. They say the name of each country as its excited athletes arrive. They flood in, the "youth of the world," answering the call from four years ago to assemble in Beijing.

I am no longer part of the "youth of the world." I am forty-five, twenty-eight years past ponytails and balance beams.

A commercial interrupts the parade of athletes. I look at the clock and think about the time. It is after 9 PM. Because of the time difference between Boston and Beijing, the opening ceremonies actually took place twelve hours ago. The program was taped for the US audience, and in truth all of this is long over.

I have been sitting in this waiting room for two hours now, and my head is pounding. My shoulders are rigid. I have to ask someone what's going on. I stand up and find that my knees are sore from sitting cross-legged on the waiting room chair. I take a deep breath, nervous to face what I might find out, and walk past the nurse seated at the reception desk. I press the metal button so many others have pressed before me tonight and watch the word *EMERGENCY* split in two as the doors slide open. A large nurse's station is located behind the doors, then a long, wide corridor lit by blinding fluorescent lights. I walk past a line of rooms with half-open doors. A man is standing in the hallway, talking on his cell phone. His shoulders are hunched, his head bent forward. He looks exhausted. "I'm in the hospital," he says into the phone. "It's my mother. She fell again."

Is our story not so unusual then? Are others living through the same hell? For months we have felt so alone.

I look for my husband. I see him standing outside one of the rooms. He is speaking to a middle-aged woman in a white lab coat. They are looking at papers on a clipboard. I approach and notice the strained expression on Jean-Paul's face. He looks up without smiling, nods quickly at me, and holds up a finger, indicating that I should wait a minute until he can explain what's going on.

"Does this mean she's being declared legally incompetent to handle her own affairs?" Jean-Paul asks. Then he adds, "Will she think I have done this to her?"

I step backward to give Jean-Paul and the doctor some space so they can talk. The motion is strangely unsteady. No Tai Chi masters move with me; no audience watches, enraptured. I am not in a stadium or bird's nest, high up and safe from the fray. I am in a hospital in Cambridge, Massachusetts, and the circle is collapsing.

# CHAPTER EIGHT

# Forty-six

It is the morning of my forty-sixth birthday. The sun just rose over the hills and painted them a watercolor pink. I am sitting in the dining room of my parents' house, the renovated upstate New York farmhouse where I grew up. If there is any place that feels like home to me, it is this house. But as I watch the sun greet the Sunday morning that brings me one year closer to fifty, I realize I have never stayed anywhere long enough to really feel at home.

Just as the sun cleared the hills, a wild rabbit appeared outside the dining-room window. The rabbit stood still, its ears twitching, closer to the house than I have ever seen a wild rabbit. I watched it for a while, contemplated the life of a rabbit, noticed that this one's wiry haunches were ready to spring into action at the first sign of danger. Sure enough, within minutes the rabbit disappeared into the bushes with a flick of its white tail. The rabbit was here, and then it was gone. I was just an observer witnessing one brief moment of its life.

I have been eating a small piece of apple pie; I baked it on Friday after Jean-Paul and I picked apples at a nearby orchard. We wandered through the rows of carefully planted trees, picked a few hard, red apples, then some green ones, then some that were both red and green. The orchard had provided us with a large, white paper bag with its logo printed on both sides, and we filled the bag with half a bushel, then sat contentedly for a while on a hillside in front of a big red barn near some other weekend harvesters, enjoying the warmth of an unexpectedly sunny day.

I really shouldn't be eating pie, and certainly not before seven in the morning. Lately I have been trying, yet again, to regain the slim young body I once had. Frankly, I have been aching to reclaim a lot of things I once had or was or felt, but I doubt I'll ever see—or be—most of them again. No matter how much I fight the truth, the Faye of yesterday seems beyond me, out of reach. I chastise myself often, telling myself if I were more disciplined about my diet, worked harder and denied myself more, the body I once had and the person I once was would reappear. So far none of it has worked, and lately I am noticing that I am tired of trying. Today is my birthday. I have watched the sun rise and have noticed a rabbit, and I am eating a slice of apple pie before seven in the morning. So be it.

I'm not sure how I feel about turning forty-six, although entertaining the topic implies I have a choice. For a number of years I have been increasingly uncomfortable on my birthday, because I am scared of getting old. As soon as I feel the fear rising, or sense my depression about the passage of time, I think about a woman I met in Oregon when I had just turned thirty. I was visiting my first husband's family. We were gathered around the dinner table with Aaron's parents and a group of their friends. The occasion was the forty-first birthday of one of the guests, and Aaron's mother dimmed the dining-room lights and entered the room carrying a festive white cake. A single candle stood in the middle, its flame reflected in the large picture windows overlooking a stand of pine trees that were outlined by the moon. We sang "Happy Birthday" as Aaron's mother placed the cake in the center of the table. The woman was tall and slim, with a delicate face and short brown hair; and she placed her hands on her heart, smiling warmly as she looked around the table at her singing friends. When the song ended she said, "Thank you so much. For me, every birthday is a victory and a blessing."

Aaron explained to me later that she had survived cancer.

Every year I try to think about my birthday that way. After all, sixteen years ago my own survival was in doubt; I was diagnosed with a potentially malignant tumor. I endured months of tests and two surgeries. What is generally said about life-threatening illness proved true for me; I stopped taking things for granted the way I did before my illness. I began to notice and appreciate small things more acutely, didn't grumble quite as much about chores or other things I preferred not to do. I don't enjoy running long distances, for example; I am short, my stride is slow, and I do not have especially strong lungs. In high school I was a sprinter on the track team, "built for speed, not endurance," as I've often been told.

Now when I don't feel like running, I remember a promise I made to God when I was sick, when the scars on my abdomen burned and I walked just five or ten minutes a day for exercise. I promised that if I was ever able to exercise for real again, I would never complain about it. I would appreciate the fact that I was alive and could move.

Now when I get bored with the road and resent the heavy, gasping feeling in my lungs, I remember that promise. I make an effort to feel my legs moving and my feet hitting the ground. I try to taste the air. If none of that makes me feel alive or grateful, I challenge myself to notice something small along the road, something I would never see if I didn't look carefully: a caterpillar on the leaf of a roadside weed, or a tree that is growing in an odd way, split in the middle. I remind myself that if I endure the run just to be done with it, if I rush through anything without experiencing it, I will miss something important.

Why, then, do I feel sad today? Shouldn't I be filled with appreciation? If I sense I am not grateful, I chastise myself and force the feeling, because it is a right feeling. Still, there is no escaping the truth this birthday represents; I am a year older, a year further away from my youth, a year closer to whatever happens after youth disappears. My sadness is mingled with fear, and I notice that the fear grows stronger every year.

When I was twenty-eight and living in Israel, I had dinner with a friend of my parents who lived in Jerusalem. I told her that I was nervous about turning thirty. She threw back her head and laughed, and said, "If you think thirty is old, wait until you turn seventy."

When I was young, I tricked myself into believing that what was true for the rest of humanity would not be true for me. I was certain I was ageless, invincible, that growing older was for people I could not relate to or understand. When I was sixteen, my mother was forty-four, and my father was forty-eight; I thought of them as older than I would ever be, at a stage in life where everything was settled and decided. Somehow I convinced myself that time would not touch me the way it touched everyone else. The future was always in front of me. Opportunities were abundant, and I would be forever youthful, my face wrinkle free, my body flexible and strong, no cellulite on my hips. I remember wondering how my body would transform from the age I was to the next. *If my body is what it is right now*, I thought, *and it will be the same tomorrow and the same the day after that, how will it ever become something different, alien, old?*

Today I am forty-six, and very little in my life is settled or decided. I can't say that this is a normal state for people my age; I seem to have gotten a bit more distracted along the way than most. I lost my ability to have children when I was sick, and my early divorce from Aaron led to a lonely decade without a partner or the opportunity to adopt. The years passed, and I never had the responsibilities taken on by friends who started families and were transformed into adults simply because they had children. I missed that phase of life, and now, despite my marriage to Jean-Paul, I admit I feel a little lost. My original road map didn't cover the territory I found myself in for much of my adult life: single, unable to have children, and constantly moving. I changed jobs often. For a long time I found myself following one road and then turning onto another, deciding randomly if the turn would be right or left, then unsure if the choice I made was the right one. Really, even now I see nothing ahead of me clearly. No brightly lit, picturesque town waits at the end of this highway.

Some people say fairy tales are deceptive and question whether such stories should be told to little girls like I was: girls who are not likely to grow up and meet handsome princes. I am divided on the issue. I do think fairy tales are deceptive. As far as I can tell after forty-six years, there are no bluebirds tying bows on ball gowns or chariots arriving to whisk me off into the magical night. True, there are wicked witches, but no prince's kiss has ever woken me from my sleep. Usually the alarm clock does. My sense is that there is happiness to be found, but it is not "ever after"—it comes in starts and stops or at unexpected moments that do not necessarily have anything to do with love. Let me reverse that. Happiness always has to do with love—but not just romantic love. Sometimes love is feeding a cat. Sometimes it's singing Abba songs with a friend in a car in Wyoming. Sometimes love just happens, in an instant, when you see something beautiful. Romantic love is more about willingness than wedding bells and destiny. Or maybe it is willingness *and* destiny, or destiny is what we choose to believe it is because we're afraid to believe that life is all about luck.

I guess I do believe that fairy tales should be told to little girls. When we are young we have a capability that is difficult to maintain in later years. Children can imagine the fantastic and believe in endless possibilities. That capacity should be fed, I think, with extraordinary things. Magical things. Why not? If we aren't allowed to believe life is beautiful when we are young, will we find anything beautiful later in life? Perhaps beauty is self-evident, but maybe it is just another thing we are taught, or choose, to believe in. Beauty, like ugliness, is a human interpretation of what exists. If our ability to believe in beautiful things is squashed when we are little girls, what will be left for us to see or discover later in life?

A short while ago Jean-Paul wandered downstairs, wondering where I was so early in the morning, and found me typing on my laptop in the dining room. My parents are away for the weekend. Jean-Paul and I came here to briefly escape from our lives, which have been stressful because we both work, I'm in school, and all the while my mother-in-law is struggling with a terminal illness. Jean-Paul entered the kitchen wearing nothing but his running shorts. I think it's fair to say that my husband is handsome; his blue eyes, dirty-blond hair, and expressive lips almost landed him the lead role in *The Blue Lagoon* opposite Brooke Shields in the 1970s. Now, however, there are deep lines around his eyes and outlining his lips. This morning, dark-red impressions were visible around his mouth where a sleep apnea mask had been pressing against his skin all night. His eyes were bloodshot and tired, and tinged with yellow due to a benign health condition common among people of French Canadian heritage.

Jean-Paul, my high-IQ husband, is a cum laude graduate of Brandeis University. He studied guitar at the Berklee College of Music when he was in his twenties and now holds a master's degree in social work. He also worked for nearly ten years as

a stripper, starting out in a show called "The Male Encounter"
at the Palace nightclub on the outskirts of Boston. Crowds of
young women arrived in stretch limousines for bachelorette
parties and were entertained by sexy men with muscles. The
women drank, cheered and laughed, and stuffed dollar tips
into the dancers' thongs. Jean-Paul grew his hair long, added
blond highlights, and performed in numerous dance acts,
including one titled "Hellvis." At the end of every show, the
young women lined up to pay five dollars for an autographed
picture.

I knew Jean-Paul from Brandeis, where I had also studied,
but hadn't seen him in seventeen years when I returned to
Boston. We met again at a party hosted by a mutual friend.
I knew nothing about Jean-Paul's unusual career. I learned
about the stripping from a hairstylist at a Boston salon Jean-
Paul recommended to me. I told the stylist who had referred
me, and he said, "Oh, you mean the Chippendales guy."

"Chippendales?" I asked in surprise, and the stylist looked
embarrassed, as if he had slipped up. It turned out Jean-Paul,
at forty, had transitioned from "The Male Encounter" into a
job as emcee of the Chippendales show on Friday nights at
the Roxy. He danced in the opening act and emceed the rest
of the show, at one point aiming his microphone out toward
the audience and asking seductively, "Is there a horny woman
in the house?"

It wasn't quite the way Prince Charming had been described, but it was interesting.

Watching my husband shuffle around the kitchen and set
up the coffeemaker, it occurred to me that the women who
once stood in line to meet him might be a little surprised to
see him now, with his tired eyes and those other-worldly red
impressions on his face. But then I thought about what he'd
said when he entered the room and found me typing. He told
me he was disappointed that I had gotten up so early, because

he had intended to bring me a cup of coffee in bed on my birthday.

Jean-Paul and I took a long walk yesterday along the back roads that climb up and down the rural, hilly landscape of my hometown. We walked from my parents' house along County Route 5, past old farming homesteads and Colonial houses, and into the center of town—an intersection marked by a blinking traffic light. We stopped for croissants at a coffee shop that now occupies the old post office, then continued on past acre after acre of old farmland flanked by woods.

Every now and then as we walked, I spied a caterpillar inching its way across the pavement from one side of the road to the other. There is little traffic on the back roads; but occasionally cars do pass, and I can never bear the thought of a caterpillar getting squashed beneath speeding tires. So each time I saw one I found a stick at the side of the road or pulled up a weed and held it in front of the caterpillar until it climbed on. Then I moved the little creature to safety on the opposite side of the road. This habit of mine makes for relatively slow progress on country walks.

At one point a car raced up over a hill after I noticed one of the caterpillars. I had no time to grab a stick, so I scooped the caterpillar into my hands and rushed it to the side of the road before the car zoomed past. I don't think I got to the next caterpillar in time, and it still bothers me to think about that as I sit here and write. I thought the caterpillar was far enough in the opposite lane to be missed by an oncoming car, but after the car passed and I picked it up and deposited it on the other side of the road, I noticed that a spot of yellow goo remained on my palm. Jean-Paul suggested that the caterpillar might have voided as a defense mechanism, as some animals do when they are frightened. But I suspect that it had been hit by the car, even though it curled into a ball the way caterpillars always do when I touch them. This thought bothers me so much sitting here that for a moment I feel paralyzed by sadness.

I know, logically, that there are caterpillars I can save and caterpillars I can't save, and that it is perhaps more than silly to attempt to save any caterpillars at all. It's not as if I control the fate of the world's creatures, or as if saving one or two or three or four makes any difference in a world populated by trillions of caterpillars. But I can't stop my impulse. Saving caterpillars makes me feel a little better about something. Perhaps I'm just playing the leading role in my own fairy tale, one in which the smallest, most insignificant beings are hugely important, and I am the hero who can rescue them all.

A few years ago I went on a whale watch off the coast of Portland, Maine. Riding in boats always makes me seasick, so I took medication before the trip to stave it off. Unfortunately it was October, the end of the whale-watching season, and the boat wandered around the harbor and the waters farther out for six hours before the captain spotted a whale for us to watch. Most of the passengers were in a good mood, excited for the outing; and they passed the long hours sitting on the deck wrapped in warm, waterproof clothing, enjoying the cold, salty sea air. Occasionally they ducked inside to buy food at a small concession stand or to sit at wooden booths indoors. Finally a humpback whale was sighted in the distance, the captain made a gleeful announcement over the PA system, and everyone rushed to the appropriate side of the boat, grabbing cameras and binoculars. My medication had long worn off, however. The boat was listing from side to side, I was nauseous, my head was pounding. We headed straight into twelve-foot swells that pushed the bow up and then brought it crashing down so that the frigid seawater sprayed over the passengers and onto the decks. Still, I stood up on shaky legs, grasped the cold railing on the side of the boat, and stared eagerly across the water. When I saw it, when I saw that whale, my head, my stomach, the cold salt spray on my face, and the icy railing under my hands didn't matter. I couldn't breathe for a moment; I felt an indescribable joy. The whale breached once, then twice, and I wrapped my frozen fingers around the small camera hanging from a strap around my neck and held it as steadily as I could, hoping to snap some pictures. The whale breached again, and I caught it on film. It breached five times, leaping from the sea and falling gracefully onto its side with a massive splash, finally disappearing for the last time beneath the surface. Then the boat turned around and headed back to shore.

I see the whale and I love the whale. I see the whale and I turn my pounding head off, I turn my thoughts off, I ignore the salty taste in my mouth and the rocking of the boat and the sound of the excited captain yelling into the microphone. In that moment there is nothing; there is no past, no future, no birth, and no death. There is just the whale. The whale is beautiful, and I believe.

Today is my birthday. I am forty-six years old, but I don't want to think about it anymore. The sun is up and I smell the coffee brewing and I have spent too much time wishing I was something I am not—wishing I was young.

The sun does not care that I am forty-six, and the hills do not care, and the caterpillars do not care, and the whale does not care, and my husband does not care; and if I'm not careful, it will all vanish in an instant, like the rabbit, and I will miss the moment we share.

# CHAPTER NINE

# Shibboleth

*Judges 12:5-6: And the Gileadites captured the fords of the Jordan against the Ephraimites. And when any of the fugitives of Ephraim said, "Let me go over," the men of Gilead said to him, "Are you an Ephraimite?" When he said, "No," they said to him, "Then say Shibboleth," and he said, "Sibboleth," for he could not pronounce it right.*

When the clouds parted beneath the plane, a blanket of streetlights appeared. They glittered in the darkness like earthbound stars. As we approached Heathrow, the lights got closer and soon surrounded the plane. The engines whined, and the landing gear made contact with the runway. I felt a jolt, a bounce, and then we were down. The plane slowed, turned, and taxied toward the gate. I glanced across the aisle at my travel companion. Amy looked tired. It was two in the afternoon back in Boston, but the flight had lasted more than six hours, and the sun had already set on this side of the Atlantic. Amy turned toward me, smiled, and gave me a thumbs-up. We had met in London as college students studying abroad twenty-six years before. I had been back to England a number of times since then, but not for the past ten years. It had become an illusion to me, like a face glimpsed briefly through curtains that had closed. But now the curtains had been thrown open, and there she was: the past, right before my eyes.

It seemed as if the travelers in the crowded terminal had arrived from every corner of the world. They wore blue jeans, trench coats, business suits, saris, African prints, burkas, turbans. Pulling our carry-on suitcases behind us, we wove through the crowd, following the signs to the Underground. We paid one-way fares at the ticket booth, took an escalator down to a steamy platform, and boarded a Piccadilly Line train.

At first we traveled aboveground. I stared out the window as the train rocked along the tracks, trying to spot something familiar in the darkness. I could make out long rows of indistinct warehouses and then brightly lit streets lined with attached redbrick homes. The traffic, distinguishable only by rows of headlights, was traveling on the left side of the roadways. Across the train car, a group of young people sported jaunty hairstyles; the men's were spiked into unruliness, and one of the women had dyed parts of her hair blue. Their jeans were glued to impossibly skinny legs. I listened to the rise and fall of their British English and remembered a time when the London accent had become so familiar that I had started to pick up some of the phrases and tones only to lose them again after I'd returned home.

Focusing on the reflection in the window opposite me, I took stock of my appearance. Small, five foot one, with a curvy but muscular build, dark eyes, and brown hair that curled haphazardly around my face. People tended to think I was younger than forty-six, but I was no longer the fresh-faced girl of nineteen who—years earlier—had first taken this train. Amy, sitting next to me, was tall and slim, with the long legs of a marathon runner. She looked so American with her wavy blond hair, blue eyes, and perfect smile. Over the years I had been mistaken for Italian, Latina, Irish, and Israeli. But at that

moment, sitting next to Amy in my relaxed-fit jeans and Sau-
cony running shoes, it was obvious I hailed from the States.

As the train rolled on, I thought about why I was here.
The decision to return to London had been somewhat spon-
taneous. A few weeks before, I'd been having dinner with a
small group of friends. Amy was sitting next to me. I turned
to her and asked, "How would you feel about a weekend trip
to London?"

"London? Let's do it," she replied without hesitation.

It wouldn't be difficult to take a few days off. Jean-Paul and
I had been married for just two years, and we were childless.
I worked at home as a freelance writer and could easily clear
my schedule.

Amy's life was also her own. She had been a social work-
er in her twenties before attending law school and then had
given up her law career to launch a dog-walking business. She
lived in Cambridge, where her business had expanded, and
now had employees who could take care of her clients when
she wanted to get away. Amy also had limitless energy; in the
past few years she'd traveled to China, Nepal, and Egypt on
her own or with friends. Never married, she now was in the
process of adopting a baby from Viet Nam. Once she got the
call that a baby was available, her life would change forever.
Until then she was up for anything.

"I would love to get away," she said.

My true motivation was also to get away. Although I had
been back in Boston for just five years, it felt like an eternity.
Since my experience in England as a college student, I had
been plagued by wanderlust. I had lived in nine cities or towns,
two states, and three countries before my first marriage, to
Aaron. After that marriage ended I went on to hold six jobs
in three different states. I told myself it was exciting to be free,
to see and experience so much. But in truth I was haunted by
a constant and intense loneliness. I always had the feeling that

something was missing from my life, and on some level I knew that whatever it was, I wouldn't stop looking until I found it.

I was forty-one when I'd met Jean-Paul, and three years later we were married. Believing that a solid love was what I'd been seeking, I experienced a profound sense of relief. We bought our house, and I thought I would finally settle down and be happy.

Within a year the restlessness had returned.

The Westland Hotel is located in a townhouse-style building on Bayswater Road in the center of London. Having emerged from the Tube onto a busy city street, Amy and I nearly missed the manicured front courtyard hidden behind a tall brick wall. Kensington Gardens, the famous London park, was situated directly across the street. This was perfect for Amy's morning runs, and I was pleased as well. I had always loved spending time in London's spacious parks, and though I could never match Amy's pace or endurance, I was looking forward to jogging in the mornings on my own.

We pushed through the hotel's glass doors into a small, carpeted foyer with a modest front desk. While Amy checked us in, I inspected the visitor's lounge located to the left of the entrance, one step down from the main floor. The space was open and inviting, offering a cozy fireplace and plush, cushioned chairs. Red curtains tied back with thick gold rope adorned large picture windows.

Back in the foyer, a carpeted staircase wound toward the upper floors, but a bellman accompanied us to the second floor in an elevator, which he referred to as "the lift." Our room was small by American standards, but I thought it was perfect for our needs. Amy didn't love the arrangement of the space (the bathroom was located down a narrow corner hallway), and she mentioned that the mattresses on the twin beds were stiff. I'm more adaptable—a side effect of having moved so often—and didn't mind the room's little quirks. Before long

Amy had embraced them as well.

Our enjoyment of the hotel didn't waver after that, although we experienced certain idiosyncrasies during our stay. The ceilings were thin, and when the guests above returned to their room at night, it sounded as if a herd of elephants had arrived. Breakfast, which was included in the price of the room, was served at the bottom of a steep, narrow staircase that led down from the foyer to the basement. The meal consisted of plain toast with butter and jam accompanied—upon request—by juice and hot coffee.

All that mattered was that the hotel was clean, affordable, and located in the center of our beloved London. All the city's attractions were at our disposal. Knowing this, we fell asleep that first night in a happy, optimistic mood.

Amy would be the first to admit that traveling with her can be likened to a stint in basic training. She is a let's-get-going, no-excuses kind of woman; and once she's on the move, all a companion can do is make chase.

On our first day we were awake by eight thirty, finished with our showers and breakfast by ten, and out the hotel door one minute after that, ready to take on London by foot.

Once we had made our way through the congested traffic that was Bayswater Road and passed through the entrance gate to Kensington Gardens, I knew I was truly back in London. Paved walkways traversed expansive green lawns and intersected near fountains capped with marble statues. Yellow daffodils and multicolored tulips bloomed in manicured gardens. Flotillas of exotic ducks and noble white swans glided on the surface of a large pond. Majestic trees lined the footpaths, and countless birds hid among their branches, filling the air with their morning songs.

I was back. My heart soared.

I worked hard to keep up with Amy, who trekked on ahead of me as I absorbed the sights and sounds of the park. We paused for a moment in front of Kensington Palace, the one-time home of Princess Diana, and again at Diana's memorial. I had seen Diana in person twice, once in Leicester Square as she entered a movie premier and once when the royal family was greeting the crowds from a Buckingham Palace balcony on the queen's birthday. It was hard to believe, even now, that Diana was gone. She had been just a year older than me.

Once Amy and I crossed Kensington Gardens we continued through the larger and more famous Hyde Park, stopping briefly now and then to snap photographs. Passersby spoke British English, French, occasionally German, and even Russian. The tones of the varied languages were foreign yet familiar, and I thirstily drank them all in.

We walked and walked through the park. Eventually the air turned cool and thick, and clouds began to gather in the sky. Amy retrieved an umbrella from my day pack, and I withdrew a light yellow raincoat. We had come prepared for the intermittent rains that are an integral part of London life.

We made the transition from Hyde Park to St. James's Park just before eleven. People were milling about in front of Buckingham Palace; we had arrived just in time to witness the Changing of the Guard. We paused for a few minutes on the edge of the crowd as the horns of a marching band sounded. Before long the red-coated regiment paraded past. The guards were stiff, formal, and straight-faced. The golden straps attached to their black hats appeared to be glued to their chins. Witnessing the pomp was fun for a few minutes, but Amy and I had both seen the Changing of the Guard before, so we didn't linger long. Instead, we pressed on toward the Thames and Big Ben.

We viewed the towering old clock and Parliament from a footbridge packed with pedestrians. I began to feel as if we were living this day inside a picture postcard; wherever we walked, a famous landmark appeared. The enormous Eye of

London—the slow-moving Ferris wheel that hadn't existed when we were college students—loomed on the opposite bank of the river. We toyed with the idea of taking a ride but decided against it after a brief wait at the end of the lengthy line. Instead, since the sky had cleared, we found a pub with outdoor seating and ordered sandwiches and two pints of lager. Devouring our meal hungrily, we watched the stately Thames flow by.

By this time I was drunk, not with lager, but with the headiness of being back in Europe. It had been years since this kind of adrenaline had coursed through my veins, quickening my breath and sharpening my senses. The reminder that there was much more to be experienced in life than the people and places of my everyday life was hitting me like a drug. There was more; there was more! I wasn't sure why I felt so excited; this was far from the first time I had traveled, after all, and I had lived in London for a year. But I felt my heart leaping in my chest as if it had been trapped inside a dark box for years, and finally the lid had been lifted.

Next on our agenda was the Tate Modern, one of London's newer museums. One would think, considering my inclination to test boundaries, that I would be a devotee of modern art. In fact, the opposite is true. When it comes to art, literature, and even music, my tastes lean decidedly toward the classic. I am enchanted by van Gogh, Rodin, and Tolstoy. I love Mozart but find myself puzzled by the dissonance evident in some modern classical music. And when it comes to rock and roll, I'm stuck in the sixties, seventies, and eighties. I appreciate dance in almost any form, but even that medium stumps me if the choreography is too angular or cryptic.

I believe my response to art reveals a rift in my sense of self. During those years when I was in constant motion, the act of relocation catered to my illusion that something better could be discovered by moving forward. Motion made life more interesting—made me more interesting—because new experiences always lay ahead. What existed in the moment was provisional, so temporary it hardly counted. I could tolerate being unhappy if whatever state I was in—literally or figuratively—wouldn't last.

When it comes to art, on the other hand, I am attracted to what stills me. I want to be lulled by the rhythm of iambic pentameter, by the flow of a straightforward narrative, by the choreographed leaps of Baryshnikov. I crave beauty that removes the manufactured excess of the human condition, leaving only what is unadorned and true. Perhaps I am seeking a kind of rescue from the distractions of modern life, or from the restless temptations of my idealistic dreams.

Still, I would never summarily dismiss any form of art. So I dutifully followed Amy into the museum. Tourists, students, and sophisticated Londoners milled around the entrance hall. They checked coats, hats, and bags in the cloakroom and slowly made their way toward the exhibits. Feeling claustrophobic in the swarming building after a morning outdoors, I was thankful our visit would be relatively short. We jostled for position in the small groups of visitors that moved like herds of cattle from work to work, room to room. I followed Amy dutifully as she perused two full floors and observed every exhibit with interest. But I found myself battling a general state of puzzlement. I appreciated the aesthetic appeal of certain pieces, responding positively, for example, to the cubist paintings, but was admittedly baffled by most of what I saw. At one point I noticed two rows of yellow bricks lined up on the floor. I stared at them uncomprehendingly.

Eventually I suggested that Amy continue without me and made my way toward a seating area on the second floor. A balcony overlooked the first level of the museum. Peering through glass windows, I stared curiously at a large installation below. It was titled *Shibboleth*, according to a nearby placard, and consisted of a room-sized enclosure with a plain concrete floor. A jagged crack ran through the middle of the floor from one side of the room to the other. That was it; that was the exhibit, a crack in a floor. I glanced through the description on the placard and learned it represented "a fracture in modernity itself." Uncertain what that meant, I backed away from the window. All the seats in the lounge were filled, so I sat cross-legged on the floor. When Amy found me an hour later, I was scribbling thoughts about the day in my notebook.

By now it was midafternoon, and Amy suggested we continue walking east toward Tower Bridge and the Tower of London. My energy was waning, but it was difficult to turn down the opportunity to see more familiar landmarks. We resumed our excursion, eventually crossing the river at the bridge. When we reached the old fortress, which once served as a royal prison, we opted out of a tour and instead browsed through the shops, elbow to elbow with other tourists. I couldn't resist purchasing the ultimate kitschy souvenir: a desktop coin bank shaped like a classic London telephone booth.

Once we had exhausted the shopping possibilities, Amy proposed we continue our trek. But by now my legs ached. I was getting tired and convinced Amy to head back to the hotel.

The narrow, winding streets—some paved with cobblestones—on the north side of the river were lined with old banks and shops and apothecaries. Eventually we found ourselves at Covent Garden Market, where we walked straight past a street performer, driven by our desire for a cold drink. Eschewing the shadowy interior of a typical British pub, we chose a brightly lit bar with a festive ambiance. The after-work crowd took up most of the barstools and round, raised tables nearby. Luckily, we found two empty spots at the bar, and Amy flagged down a bartender and ordered margaritas. Mine tasted sugary and cool, and because fatigue and hunger were now taking hold, I drank it a little too quickly. By the time we stepped back onto the street, I felt slightly unsteady. But we still had several miles to go.

Seven hours after we'd left the Westland Hotel we fell through the front doors into the foyer. "London in a day," Amy laughed once we were upstairs and had flopped, face-first, onto our beds. I thought I might pass out on the spot. My feet were killing me.

"No one ever wants to travel with me again after the first day," Amy said.

"I can see why," I replied, my face buried in a pillow. But I couldn't help noticing that for the first time in months, I felt completely, thrillingly, alive.

At eleven that night, when Jean-Paul would be returning from work back in Boston, I ventured out to the pay phone across the street. I pulled the door of the booth closed amid the old, familiar odors of musty air, steel, and traces of urine. An AT&T operator put through my call, and then Jean-Paul was on the other end of the line. He was happy to hear my voice. He told me everything was fine at home and listened as I described what it felt like to be back in London. Jean-Paul is not much of a traveler, and although we had been to Mexico, Puerto Rico, and Bermuda since our marriage, he had never crossed an ocean in his life.

"Have fun," he said. "I'll be at the airport when you get back."

"Goodnight," I replied, and hung up. I stepped out of the phone booth, breathed in the city air, and watched the late-night traffic roll by.

When I awoke Saturday morning, the first thing I noticed was a dull ache that radiated from my shins. Then I felt the burn of new blisters on my feet. Amy was already gone. Attempting to ignore the pain, I eased my legs off the bed and changed from an oversize t-shirt and shorts into my running clothes. I washed, secured my hair in a ponytail, and stepped out for a jog in the park.

The morning air felt cool on my face, and I stuffed my hands, which get cold easily, into the pockets of my sweatshirt. After entering the park, I fell in love with Kensington Gardens all over again. The sun burned its way through an early-morning fog as traffic hummed on the streets surrounding the park. Quickening my pace from a walk to a jog, I passed solitary Londoners wrapped in tidy trench coats walking their small dogs. Sometimes they stopped to watch the dogs frolic in the sweet-smelling, freshly cut grass. Birdsong rained down from above as the exercise eased the stiffness in my legs. My breathing was hard but steady. After a while I looked up, smiled at the sky, and noticed a sensation I hadn't experienced in some time—it felt something like joy.

On our second full day in London, Amy and I took our morning runs and then made plans for a stop at the British Museum, a walk through Regent's Park, and a visit to the London Zoo. We decided, once again, to do our sightseeing on foot.

Refueled by our toast and coffee, we merged onto the crowded sidewalks and headed toward Bloomsbury, stopping briefly at Harrods department store in the boroughs of Kensington and Chelsea. The world-renowned shopping mecca was packed with eager customers who jostled through vast halls stocked with fresh foods, furniture, clothing, cosmetics, and endless other products in seemingly every category. Overcome by the busy tumult, we only dabbled in two of the first-floor halls, eying English chocolates and other tempting foods before leaving and heading off to the British Museum.

It is impossible to do the museum justice in one visit, so once we arrived at the sprawling building, with its neoclassic columns, we decided to focus on one or two exhibits. We found the Parthenon's Elgin Marbles—which I had studied in a class on ancient Greek art—and visited the mummies in the Egyptian rooms. Every aspect of the massive building felt familiar: the marble stairways, the echo of the cavernous halls, the antiquities lined up carefully beneath shiny glass enclosures. But our schedule was packed, and we stayed for only an hour before exiting and continuing north toward Regent's Park.

The British and European Studies Group, which had organized our study abroad program, has long since closed its doors. But in our student days it was headquartered in a tony neighborhood called York Terrace East on the southern edge of Regent's Park. We recognized the area, with its stucco houses and broad, graceful streets. After a quick lunch at a pub furnished with dartboards and pool tables, we crossed the street and entered the park.

Regent's Park holds special meaning for me. During my first three months in London, before Amy and the other second-semester students arrived, I took weekly walks alone through the park, crossing between our school and the London Zoo. I was taking courses in English literature and theatre arts, and one of the drama teachers required each student to observe an animal at the zoo on a regular basis and then perform as that animal in class. I chose to study some lemurs from Madagascar, who looked like living, breathing, teddy bears. I was enchanted by their soft, brown bodies and wide, surprised eyes. I watched how they clung to the branches of their forest habitat as if letting go to the one thing that was safe and familiar would cause them to lose their balance. When it was my turn to perform, I transformed myself into a lemur in a matter of seconds.

Continuing north on one of the sprawling pedestrian avenues, we passed an array of sports fields and flower gardens, ignoring the dark clouds that were sweeping across the sky. Without warning, those clouds unleashed a violent downpour, forcing us to dash into the first building we saw. We found ourselves dripping in the doorway of a park café among a small group of Londoners who had gotten the same idea. We bought two cups of hot coffee and stood near the windows, watching the rain hammer on the glass. When the storm had passed, we continued on to the zoo.

The London Zoo was somewhat disappointing. We saw llamas, monkeys, and lions before crossing a footbridge to a large enclosed aviary located on the opposite side of Regent's Canal. But the general state of the zoo, and the limited size of the enclosures, disturbed us. We were especially troubled by the fish aquariums, which appeared to be seriously neglected. Without staying long, we decided on an alternate route back to Notting Hill through the neighborhoods of Little Venice and St. John's Wood.

That night, over dinner at an Italian restaurant near the hotel, I asked Amy about her family back home. I knew her parents had divorced when Amy was fifteen and that her mother now lived at the shore, north of Boston.

"I called her to ask if I should visit on Easter, but she told me she was going for a bike ride," Amy said with a shrug.

I was surprised to learn that Amy's father was actually in London that same weekend. "He's really busy, and I'm not sure which hotel he's staying in," Amy said.

I suddenly recalled a moment from the first day of our trip when Amy had paused in front of a large hotel near the Thames. She had stared at the front door for a moment, and then, without a word, had turned away and moved on.

On our last day in London, my feet hurt so badly when I woke up in the morning that I hobbled unsteadily as I moved about the room. According to the map that had been guiding us through the city, we had walked twelve miles on each of the first two days, all on paved pathways, and hard cement sidewalks. Even Amy admitted that her legs were sore. Still, we prepared for our early exercise. I was determined to spend one last morning in Kensington Gardens.

My jog lasted just twenty minutes. My legs were exhausted, and I simply couldn't do more. I felt an odd sense of mourning as I strolled past the pond and watched the ducks. They slid peacefully across the water that glinted in the morning light. My heart ached when I noticed two dogs rolling in the grass as their guardians stood careful watch nearby. I tilted my face up toward the sunlight, and suddenly an unexpected word burst into my thoughts: *stay*.

*Stay*. The word seemed as foreign to me as the Tate Modern or the Elgin Marbles. *Go* was the word that usually invaded my consciousness. *Stay* was a shock, but I heard it unmistakably, as if a child running next to me was crying it out while tugging at my sweatshirt. I tried to calm my breathing, which was still labored from the jog. Then the full weight of a heavy fatigue hit me hard, and I understood that it was a feeling that had been with me far longer than the past two days.

"Stay," the voice said. "Stay in Europe. Come home."

In April 1983, during a four-week break from my studies in London, I'd traveled around "the continent" with some friends. Armed with backpacks, a tourist guide called *Let's Go Europe!*, British currency, and American traveler's checks, we'd visited France, Monaco, Italy, Greece, Austria, and Holland, spending half our nights sleeping on trains.

Because we had been living in Great Britain for six months, we qualified to purchase European Inter-rail passes. Unlike the American Europass, the Inter-rail pass included access to trains that traveled behind what was then known as the "Iron Curtain." Out of curiosity we took a detour from Vienna to Budapest, which at that time was still under communist rule.

Budapest was a gray, dreary place. Red stars were conspicuous on every building and sign, and huge statues of Marx and Engels had been installed in the center of the city. Soldiers combed the streets; security was tight. The Hungarian people seemed to move in slow motion, hands stuffed into pockets, heads bent toward the ground. Tired and hungry after walking around the city, we stopped at a cafeteria-style restaurant and loaded up our trays with food. The entire meal cost the equivalent of four dollars. After sitting down and glancing at the tables around us, we suddenly felt uncomfortable about the bounty on our plates. Every person in the restaurant had purchased just one bowl of soup or perhaps a simple sandwich.

Hungary isn't Poland, but it was the closest I would get to the country where my father had been a child before his family was ghettoized and deported. The city felt dark, damaged, and terribly sad beneath the beauty of its imprisoned architecture. I was relieved when we left after just one day.

We returned to Vienna and then passed through Innsbruck on the way to Amsterdam, our last stop before England. When our train crossed the border into Germany late at night, a conductor passed through the car and asked to see our passports. He smiled when he noticed that our group was American and said, in a thick German accent, "You American? Me Luftwaffe!" Then he curled his hands into fists and shook them, as if he were shooting a gun on a German air force plane. "*Boom, boom, boom!*" he said, laughing, thinking he was offering us some good-hearted ribbing.

When I fell asleep a short time later, I had nightmares.

At some point, while remembering all this, I had stopped walking. The word *stay* no longer echoed through my brain. I took one last look around Kensington Gardens and then slowly made my way back to the hotel.

The streets of South Kensington seemed both foreign and familiar. I had remembered Kensington High Street as a soaring, slick business district, but the street was centered in a residential neighborhood and lined with modest markets and a few clothing shops. When Amy and I turned onto Earl's

Court Road, only the vaguest of impressions jogged my memory. I recalled the curve of the street and the white limestone buildings fronted by wrought iron fences. The area felt grungy; I remembered the grunge.

We spotted a sign that said LEXHAM GARDENS, indicating the street where we had once lived. I recognized nothing until we came across Lexham House, the building that had housed the two-bedroom flat we'd shared with two other students. Its plain brick facade looked out of place next to the traditional Georgian architecture surrounding it. Amy and I cried out and laughed with delight as we realized we were standing where we had met a quarter of a century before. We exchanged cameras and posed in front of the building.

Then an odd thing happened. Just after Amy snapped a picture of me standing in front of Lexham House, a message flashed across my camera's screen indicating that the memory card was full. The moment I took Amy's photo, her camera's battery ran out.

Our trip to the past was done.

The next morning I flew back to Boston, alone. Amy had decided to spend one more day in London and to fly back later that evening. My flight of seven hours seemed exceedingly long. I watched a movie I can't remember, ate a typical airline lunch, and recorded observations from the trip on my laptop.

After five or six hours I looked up at the video screen mounted on the wall in front of the first row of seats. Our jet was depicted as a simple white plane flying above the blue ocean. Land had just appeared to the west. Soon we would pass over Nova Scotia, turn south, and head back toward Boston.

I thought about Jean-Paul. He would be waiting at Logan Airport, at the gate or baggage claim. I would make my way through passport control and customs, a quick and easy process once I was back in the United States. I would search for my husband in the crowd, and when I saw him I would quicken my pace. Then I would step over the crack in the floor and reach out for the branch that I knew.

# CHAPTER TEN

# Morning and Night

It is early September, and lately I find that I'm sleeping through the hours when I would be happiest awake. The changing cycles of daylight catch me off guard. My head is still heavy on my pillow when the sun comes up, and leans against the couch before midnight.

The day is full of promise before the neighborhood wakes. When I get up early, I can watch from the kitchen window while dawn unfolds as if an artist is painting the sky. Cherry red dissolves over a moody gray canvas. Pink peeks over the rooftops. The canvas slowly brightens to blue. The pink fades and stretches, blue mixes with white, gentle wisps of clouds appear. A flock of Canadian geese crosses the sky, honking and breaking the silence.

I feel privileged to witness nature's birth of morning; but as I relish the feeling, a car passes by, then a neighbor steps outside and yells to his wife. His voice slices the cool morning air like a knife. My husband wakes and descends the staircase, seeking vitamins in kitchen cabinets. Two young girls burst from a door across the street. The door clatters shut. The girls run up the hill, call to each other, and laugh. They're late for the school bus. I look back at the sky, but the colors are gone.

Daytime and people merge together to become one: the piercing light of sun and eyes. Voices are like the snarling demands of wolves. Garbage trucks growl, FedEx pulls up. Brakes screech. Teenagers laugh and throw stones as they walk up the street. A machine blows leaves, or cuts down a tree. A car passes by with the bass from the radio turned up loud.

I spend the day with ears raised and eyes wide, running and hiding, searching for a meadow full of lilies. This is not the fault of others. It is I; I am wax. When forced to interact, I lose my shape.

*Ba-boom, ba-boom, ba-boom.*

Late at night I slip outside, when the people are back in their houses. The cars and trucks have stopped rumbling up the street. Finally alone with the world again, I listen for the sounds of night. Crickets sing with their wings, and an owl's distant hoot floats across the neighborhood. A cat materializes at the corner of the house, trots in silhouette across the yard. I watch it appear, then disappear. The cat is headed to quiet places, around the edges of worn-out fences, under parked cars, into the secrets of alleyways, past painted porches and the hidden things that live beneath them. I cannot follow.

Above the telephone lines that scar the sky, a patch of dark velvet makes space for the moon. If I stand outside long enough with my face tilted upward, I can convince myself that I am alone. The intrusions of neighborhood life disappear. For a moment, I am part of the night: the crickets, the owl, the moon, the cat. There are no people, no wires, no doors that slam shut. I can wander through my mind unseen. I am free, if shrouded in shadows.

The feeling won't last. Dawn will return to be followed by day, when whoever I am, or whatever I feel, is always interrupted.

# CHAPTER ELEVEN

# Into the Vacuum

The only place to sit in my mother-in-law's room at the nursing facility is on a wheelchair that belongs to her. I feel uncomfortable, so I perch on the edge of the cushioned black seat. My neck and shoulders ache with the kind of tension that pulls me forward into a slump. I am not happy to be here, but neither is Judith.

She lies in her propped-up hospital bed, her right arm moving slowly. She leans forward, reaches with her hand, and lifts a piece of pecan pastry off a roll-up table next to the bed. Slowly, she brings the sticky sweet to her mouth. Judith has made little eye contact since my husband, Jean-Paul, and I entered the room. We think the brain tumor has progressed. This sudden state of emotional absence, though hard to bear, is strangely better than the way things have been. At least she isn't ignoring us out of anger and blame.

She was crazed just four days ago in a meeting with the staff. She has been here since suffering a bad fall in her home several weeks ago; they won't release her until conditions at the house are safe. "Traitor!" she yelled at Jean-Paul during the meeting. She was enraged at his admission that she could afford the home care required for her release. Medicare covers health-related necessities but not custodial care. Judith had claimed to be destitute, an outright lie, because she was determined not to pay for any services. "I worked all my life!" she screamed, referring to the thirty years she taught art in a public school near Boston. "Someone else should pay for all this!" She stared into space, swaying back and forth in her wheelchair, her eyes round and vacant. "You're no longer my son," she finally said. "You're on your own, on your own."

Sitting here now, I feel alone, too. I struggle with emotions that are jumbled together in my head: compassion, despair, my own anger. This woman, who is both physically and mentally ill, has held us captive with her fate and her pain. She has called at all hours, made crazy demands, shrieked when things didn't go her way. After weathering the unreasonable rants for so long, I am suspicious at their absence from this room. Like a traumatized child, I wait for the storm.

Judith seems so calm and cooperative now. She lies in that bed, staring wide-eyed at a flat-screen TV that sits on a chest of drawers near the wall. Jean-Paul brought the TV from her house and set it up for her here in the room. Images flicker on it twenty-four hours a day.

Every Sunday for the past year, Judith has wanted pecan rolls from her favorite bakery. If we arrived at her house without the rolls, she turned her back on us and said, "I guess a pecan roll was too much to ask."

Now she is eating the roll we brought, slowly moving her arm up and down. She tells her son, in a slightly slurred voice, that it tastes "really good."

I glance at Jean-Paul, and my throat tightens when I see the look on his face. My husband is smiling so broadly that deep wrinkles have formed near his mouth and his eyes. He glows with pleasure at his mother's approval. For so long, nothing he has done has earned even a whisper of thanks.

The tumor that paralyzed Judith at age sixty-eight will almost certainly soon take her life. I am surprised that the thought crosses my mind so objectively. When the tumor bled and caused swelling in the brain after the biopsy, it took away everything Judith loved about her life. She woke up to the worst possible news. The tumor was malignant, the surgeon could not remove it, and whatever time she had left would be spent badly disabled.

"To think," she said later, still in shock from the news, "that I will never walk into the supermarket again, never reach down and feel the fresh apples." Her right hand made a circular gesture, and her fingers curled into arcs, as if she could still feel the apples' smooth skin. Tears slid down her face.

Thoughts of apples and supermarkets are now long gone. I wonder if Judith even knows what she is watching on TV. Usually she tunes into the latest case on Court TV or endless reruns of *Law and Order*. Now she is staring at an infomercial about a vacuum cleaner. She seems to hang on every word.

I turn toward the screen and watch for a while. A gray-haired man in a business suit touts the benefits of the Shark Cordless VX3. A pretty woman with shoulder-length hair listens, smiling. The machine is lightweight. It has swivel steering and a cordless, "go-anywhere" design, the man says. "Notice how the folding 'Backsaver' handle makes it easy to clean under a table, or even under the bed! You can finally be free of those annoying power cords!"

I have noticed something about myself as I sit in this room, which smells strongly of urine and ammonia. I rarely look at Judith. I stare at the floor, at the chest of drawers or the sink, at the hand sanitizer and paper towel dispensers hanging on the wall. I do everything I can to avoid being present with what is happening here. Knowing this makes me feel guilty, but I sense that I am protecting myself. I don't know how to handle the debilitated state of this once vibrant woman. I am afraid if

I look at her and she looks back at me, she will see the fear of death in my eyes.

Judith has accused us of thinking her hideous, but it is she who thinks this is true. A slim, uncommon beauty all her life, she hasn't coped well with the changes in her body and face. Her left leg and arm lie motionless on the bed, and her right arm has lost muscle tone. Her abdomen swells oddly, and translucent skin hangs from her bones. Her sister once told me that when Judith was young, she refused to go to school if her hair wasn't perfect. Now that same hair is oily and matted because the aides don't wash it often enough. Dark roots show through blond hair dye that Judith applied for a while at home. Her cheeks are round like small melons, swollen from steroids. Without the bright-colored lipstick she wore every day, her lips are pale and dry. Her brown eyes are wide-open; they stare a little wildly.

Despite all this, Jean-Paul has never thought of his mother as hideous. She has never been anything to him but his mom. Even before she was ill she was difficult—kind but self-centered, intelligent but condescending, unusually creative but subtly controlling. Jean-Paul loved her through that, and he loves her through this. He didn't comment when her hair fell out, or when it grew back in odd patches after chemotherapy and radiation. He didn't care how she looked when her five-foot, nine-inch frame dropped to one hundred and ten pounds. His only fear was that these were signs he was losing her, signs the drugs weren't working.

"So the pastry is good, Mom?" Jean-Paul asks again now, casting around for something to say, some way to continue connecting with her. Despite how painful every day has been since the diagnosis, he does not want to lose his mother. She continues to stare at the TV but nods, and I see satisfaction again on his face. He has pulled his chair closer, right next to her bed, and he leans in to wipe stray crumbs from her shirt.

Sitting safely apart in a corner of the room, I feel ashamed of my inability to participate. I'm the woman who rescues stray cats, clears snow off my elderly neighbors' car. Why am I hanging back now, doing nothing?

"Do you believe in an afterlife?" Judith once asked me before she got sick. "I don't," she said. "I think after this, we're just nothing."

I do believe in some form of God. Or maybe I just have hope. I wonder about the difference. Lately at night, when I wake from a bad dream, I sit straight up and feel blind. I can't see anything in the darkness around me, and my heart beats fast with the fear of death. I gulp for air but can't seem to draw anything into my lungs. I try to calm down; I tell myself death is beyond my control. I can't change it and can't understand it. Fear rushes around my body like wind, and I do what I can to push through it. Sometimes I think about something very silly. What will happen on the soap opera I don't admit to still watching? If I could write the next scene, what would the main characters say? I lie back down, rest my head on the pillow, and close my eyes. I picture the actors speaking words I put in their mouths. The handsome young man with the ragged brown hair tells the sweet young woman with blue eyes that he loves her. She smiles as tears roll down her cheeks. I comfort myself by directing the scene; I make it turn out the way I desire. I control everything on the stage of my mind. I write the endings I want.

Judith controls virtually nothing now. The last thing she held on to was the power to decide how her money was spent. Now, in her eyes, they have taken that away, too.

I think I know the day it all changed, the day something inside me broke, or just froze. Judith was living at home, in a wheel-chair; her health had been stable for a time. The chemotherapy had been effective for a number of months, and the tumor was not yet progressing. Jean-Paul and I were handling most of her needs—her shopping, her cleaning, her doctors' appointments.

Judith had called Jean-Paul while he was at work in his office and asked him to pick up a prescription at the pharmacy. She needed to take the medication at eight o'clock the next morning. Jean-Paul's workplace is an hour from her house. He couldn't leave work or get to the house that evening, but promised to have the pills delivered by the pharmacy early the next day.

Judith had slammed down the phone. She was furious that her son hadn't come when she called. She wanted that medication, and she wanted it now. She picked up the phone again and this time dialed me. I had been working in my office at home. Sobbing into the receiver, Judith told me she was out of her medication and Jean-Paul wouldn't help her. She didn't mention that he had arranged for the pharmacy to deliver the pills.

Rain was pounding the yard and street outside my house. Judith's Cambridge home was a half hour drive away. It was nearing five o'clock, rush hour. Heavy traffic would be clogging the streets around Boston. I had a terrible headache; in fact, I'd had a headache twenty-four hours a day for six months. But I heard the panic and fear in Judith's voice, and I thought she was desperate. I couldn't risk her missing important medication; I didn't want to be responsible for endangering her health. I told her I'd come. She sobbed into the phone with relief and told me, through tears, that she loved me.

I grabbed my raincoat and ran out to my car. I drove to her pharmacy through the heavy rain. Traffic was fierce; the trip took twice as long as it should have. I hit every red light between my house and Cambridge. The prescription was waiting when I got to the pharmacy; I paid for it and continued on to Judith's house. When I pulled into the driveway, the rain running down my windshield looked like the underside of a waterfall. I pushed open the car door and dashed to the front of the house, fumbled to open the lock with my spare key, and almost fell through the doorway to get out of the rain.

I had expected to find Judith desperate and tearful, thankful for the delivery of her life-saving meds. Instead, she was a few feet away from the front door, rolling her wheelchair calmly toward the kitchen. Her hair had been styled and blow-dried; her face was made up with fire-engine-red lipstick and heavy eye shadow. There was no evidence of tears, just a look of satisfaction that her wishes had been fulfilled. She barely glanced at the bag in my hand.

"So what do you think of this election?" she asked, referring to the presidential race between Senators John McCain and Barack Obama. I stood in her doorway, my head aching, rain dripping off my coat, forming small pools on the floor. Maybe I should have understood that all she needed was a sense of control. Maybe I should have considered the possibility that she was lonely and just wanted company. After all, this woman had been told she was dying. But for the first time since Judith was diagnosed with brain cancer, I felt completely enraged.

The dramatic change in Judith's condition started a couple of days ago. Last-ditch chemotherapy is making no difference; she is clearly getting worse. She can no longer get in and out of bed or maneuver her wheelchair at all. A half sister, Joanne, has offered to come from Missouri to live in the house and help care for her.

Looking at Judith now, so placid, it is hard to believe she is the woman who has been ranting for so many months. It is even harder to remember the attractive, quirky woman she was before the brain tumor. I recall just a little from the short time I knew her and from what others have told me she was like. On holidays she cooked huge meals—turkey with stuffing, green bean casserole from an old Campbell's soup recipe, warm fresh bread, and blueberry pie. She made her own jewelry—thick silver rings with precious stones glued in. She wore Ray Ban sunglasses and tight leather pants, and loved animal print shirts. Her paintings were abstract and colorful. Many of the paintings featured faces. Sometimes they stared out of a foreboding, dark gloom.

The infomercial is still on TV. "Look at that!" the woman exclaims as the vacuum sucks dirt from a cream-white carpet. "It picks up dirt; it even picks up glass!" The Shark rolls over a neat row of broken glass. When it pulls back, the glass is gone.

Jean-Paul moves his chair closer to his mother's bed. He leans over to retrieve more crumbs from Judith's shirt. She does not appear to notice. He pats her arm tenderly, asks a third time if she liked the pecan roll. His face glows again when she nods slightly and says, "It tasted great."

It occurs to me that since Judith's original diagnosis, all three of us have been afraid. Two of us have been angry. But only one of us has had the courage to hold on to love, no matter how much it hurts at the end.

# CHAPTER TWELVE

# Message from a Blue Jay

*The world is afflicted with death and decay;*
*therefore the wise do not grieve, knowing the*
*terms of the world.*

—Old Buddhist teaching

The raindrops sounded like muffled machine-gun fire as they hit the hard-packed snow. It's not supposed to rain in January, at least not in Massachusetts; but raining it was, and hard. I could shake my fist at the weather all day, but I knew it wouldn't change a thing. I would still be on this campus, huddled in my old red ski parka with the hood tied tight around my head, making my way toward a class in the rain. The scene was so cold, and damp, and dreary, and sad that I wasn't surprised when my thoughts turned to Judith.

My mother-in-law had been dead just three weeks, and one image from her final days haunted me. She was lying on her back in a hospital bed that had been wheeled into the center of her living room. The top half of the bed was slightly raised. Judith's head lay motionless on the pillow, and her face, swollen from steroids, was framed by hair dyed blond but with long, dark roots. It was difficult to look at her hair, which once had been so meticulously styled. Judith would have been mortified to see it so flat and matted. I heard her voice saying the word in my head, with an accent left over from her Missouri childhood: *martified*.

Judith's eyes were focused on the ceiling, while her mouth hung half open. I stood at the bedside, my hands clutched together so tightly that my fingers hurt. I forced myself to look at her face. I tried to remember the woman she was before brain cancer—tall and slim, elegant, cynical, obsessed with her appearance to the point of numerous plastic surgeries, emotionally fragile, a brilliant artist, eccentric. She had loved high-profile court cases and performing jury duty. Her house always seemed to be under construction; she built a second-floor deck on the back by herself, sinking wooden posts into the ground and securing them with cement. She pasted van Gogh prints onto the doors of her kitchen cabinets, altered them to her taste with her own oil paints, and then covered them with a thick, clear lacquer to make them shine. When a friend Judith had known through thirty years of teaching bought a Lexus convertible in her retirement, Judith purchased a Porsche Boxster. She was competitive and demanding, difficult but alive, in constant interaction with the world around her. Her sketches, paintings, and massive batiks—shocks of bright color that danced through lines and patterns that Judith had shaped—still crowded the walls of the living room.

Did any of it matter now, I wondered. Judith would never be that person again. She would never lift another paintbrush or climb back into her sports car, never see the next indie matinée in Harvard Square. For twenty-two months she had battled this disease while losing both her body and mind. And as I stood there, I realized that nothing I had said, or done, or felt during that time had made one bit of difference.

Judith's brown eyes swiveled toward my face. I didn't know if she could still see me or understand what she saw, but I held her gaze for as long as I could. I was afraid turning away would mean I had abandoned her. She stared at me for a while, her eyes blank, revealing nothing before they turned back toward the ceiling. It was the last time Judith ever looked at me.

The icy rain battered my red parka and trickled down the sides. As I made my way along the wet, paved path, it occurred to me that I didn't know who I was anymore. I didn't know how to keep living after watching someone die. For two years I had felt powerless. I had lost, day by day, the sense that there was any purpose to my life. Yet I couldn't just stop existing because there seemed to be no reason; and here I was, walking to class on a cold, rainy day as if whatever I might learn or accomplish there was important, as if anything about me or my life mattered.

The path to the library intersected a narrow road that circled the college campus. I stopped and felt my legs getting colder as the rain seeped through my jeans and socks. I looked to the right and left to be sure no cars were coming. None of the other students from the ten-day writing residency I was attending were in sight, and the school's full-time students were away on winter break. The misty campus was eerily quiet except for the sound of the rain hitting the frozen, steaming snow, and catching on the needles of the towering pine and fir trees that overlooked the path.

I was about to step into the road when I noticed something strange. A blue jay was standing in the middle of the path on the opposite side of the road. The bird stood stock-still in the pouring rain and looked intently at me. I stared back, confused to see a wild bird, on the ground, in the rain. Its bright-blue plumage seemed to defy the dreariness of the day, even though the tuft of feathers on top of its head had been flattened in the downpour and lay bedraggled against the bird's head and neck.

I assumed the jay would take flight once confronted with

the presence of a human being. I looked in both directions again to make sure no cars were approaching and, seeing nothing, stepped out into the empty road. To my surprise, when I looked across the road again, the blue jay was still there. In fact, it was now hopping toward me. I was so astonished by this strange behavior that I stopped short in the middle of the road and watched the bird. I instinctively moved to the left as it came close, as if to let a fellow pedestrian pass. The jay uncannily moved to its left also and turned its head as it passed to keep its eyes fixed on mine.

For weeks I had struggled to be present in my life, but now, in an instant, I was here. A blue jay had appeared on a cold, moody day, and suddenly my mind was focused. Thoughts about what lay behind or ahead of me disappeared; I even forgot to think about the rain. The blue jay's eyes remained locked on mine as it hopped toward the side of the road from which I had just come, and we were still watching each other when I felt, more than saw, the headlights.

A car approaching from the right slowed, and then stopped, probably because I was standing in the middle of the crosswalk. It was unlikely the car had stopped because of the bird; I wasn't sure if the driver could even see it in the heavy rain. Windshield wipers swished rhythmically back and forth as the driver waited. I glanced at the car, then back at the bird. The blue jay still stared at me, having stopped about two feet away, still in the middle of the road despite the arrival of the car and its engine, which idled noisily in the rain. I looked at the car again but could not make out the face of the driver behind the windshield. I was afraid that if I got out of the road and the blue jay remained still, the car would hit the bird. So I stood there, not knowing what to do, in the middle of the crosswalk, with the driver patiently waiting.

In desperation, I spoke to the blue jay.

"Look, you have to go," I told the bird, my voice urgent.

The rain was pummeling down now, threatening to drown us as well as the waiting car. I believed the car would not risk hitting me, but I was not as confident the same could be said of the blue jay. An impulse to protect the bird swelled inside me, and with it came an unexpected euphoria; I realized I was in control. As long as I did not move, that car could not move. I had power over something; I could protect this blue jay.

"Please move, or fly away, so the car doesn't hit you," I said. I backed away with slow steps and was relieved when the jay hopped far enough in the opposite direction to let the car pass between us. A stab of loss shot through me when the bird disappeared behind the car. But after it passed by, the bird was still there.

I was dumbfounded and began to wonder if the blue jay was injured or sick. Speaking aloud again, I asked, "Are you hurt? Is everything okay?"

The bird continued to stare at me. It occurred to me that if anyone found me like this, they would think I was insane. I was standing still in the middle of the road, rain rolling off my parka, soaking my jeans and boots, and talking to a blue jay.

Still, the bird didn't move. I began to plot how to handle things if the blue jay was indeed injured. Doing nothing was out of the question. I had been rescuing stray and wounded creatures for as long as I could remember, bringing home cats from dairy barns and bowling alleys, saving rabbits from a college laboratory, protecting baby birds that had fallen from their nests. I couldn't abandon a wounded blue jay and let it freeze to death or be hit by a car amid rivers of rain. Should I chase the bird toward some sort of shelter? I wondered. Should I attempt to pick it up? Was I going to miss my class?

Then things moved from strange to bizarre. The blue jay, without breaking eye contact during any of my increasingly panicked thoughts, started hopping back toward me. I looked around wildly, in case another car was coming, and then took a step forward and started to plead with the bird. "You have to go back the other way," I said. "You have to get out of the road. You could get hit by a car. You could get hurt. Can't you fly?"

The bird skipped steadily toward me before stopping just a few inches from my feet. We were back to standing in the middle of the road, staring at each other. One thing seemed certain at this point: it was my responsibility to save this bird. I knew this without question, the way I knew my own name. I looked up and surveyed the branches of the tall trees, then the road and the length of the path, trying to determine my next move. The rain pounded everything around us. Finally I looked back at the blue jay, and something odd occurred to me. Was there another way I could get this bird to move?

"Are you here to tell me something?" I asked it.

The bird took one more hop, and landed on my foot.

I was ten or eleven in the mid-1970s, growing up in rural upstate New York. My friend Peggy was a year younger than me and lived a quarter of a mile up the road. We met often on our bikes to play a special game. The game took place in a world we created, a transformed version of the world around us, complete with made-up locations and characters, and our own private archnemesis. I remember every detail of the game, every character and event. I recall these things more clearly than I remember almost anything else from my childhood—anything that you might call real.

It was a fall afternoon, after school. I was riding down the steep dirt road that served as the driveway for the old reno-vated farmhouse where my family lived, losing control of my light-green banana seat bike. The tires skidded against the dirt as I bounced down the road, and the front wheel wobbled back and forth. Rocks shot out from underneath the bike. I gripped the plastic handlebars hard while my arms and legs absorbed every jolt. I knew I had to slow down before I reached the bottom of the hill to avoid shooting straight across County

Route 5, hitting the ditch on the other side, flying over the handlebars, and smacking into a gravestone in the cemetery across the road. So I stood upright on the pedals and braked as hard as I could by pushing backward with my right foot. The rear wheel slipped slightly to the right, the bike slowed down, and I was back in control, bumping steadily down the road.

At the bottom of the hill, where the dirt road met Route 5, I stopped and planted my feet on the ground. I looked to the right and left to be sure no cars were coming. To the right, Route 5 ran alongside the large field in front of our house, where a local farmer still harvested hay for his cows. It followed a slight incline for about an eighth of a mile before disappearing over a hill. To the left, the road sloped slightly downward before bending around a corner and up a hill that was heavily shaded by red, yellow, and orange autumn leaves.

Not many cars passed this way, but when they did, they came up suddenly, speeding from either direction without warning. I listened carefully as I stared each way before hopping back onto the pedals and crossing to the other side. I rode left, glancing into the woods along the side of the road as I passed, watching for squirrels, rabbits, moles, and butterflies.

When I came to the spot where the road curved and the hill began, I climbed off my bike and rested it against my waist. I watched the top of the hill carefully, my left hand shielding my eyes as I squinted into the afternoon sun. It took just a few minutes for Peggy to appear. She was on her pink bike, and the long plastic tassels that hung from her handlebars streamed toward her face in the wind. When Peggy saw me, she stopped and climbed off her bike. She raised her right hand and waved it twice in a huge, slow arc. I returned the wave. Then we did the same thing with the opposite hands before nodding our heads in an exaggerated way, up and down twice, and burying our faces in our hands. This was our secret greeting. Now the game could begin.

Peggy sailed down the hill, her long, light-brown pigtails riding the wind. She slowed as she passed so I could pull up next to her and we could continue the ride side by side. She called out, "We have to keep the formula hidden from Movie-Man."

She was referring to a scientific formula we had scribbled on a baby doll's diaper to hide it from our nemesis.

"You're right," I called back, turning my front wheel to the right and left, playing with the tires and the pavement as I weaved alongside Peggy. Movie-Man was scary and evil. If he ever caught us, the consequences would be dire.

"He's really been after us this week," I said, raising my voice so Peggy could hear me as she rode on ahead. "I saw him at school this afternoon. He was watching my class!"

"He's definitely closing in," Peggy called over her shoulder. "If we don't move the formula to a new spot, he just might find it today."

I considered our options. "Do you think we should contact Headless and Leafbottom?" I asked, referring to Headless, who was just a big head, and Leafbottom, who had no head at all but a body completely made of leaves.

"We could do that," Peggy said, "or…we could do something Movie-Man would never expect." She paused dramatically as our bicycles glided along the road.

"Like what?" I asked.

Peggy was quiet for a moment as our bikes coasted and then slowed over the last tenth of a mile to the cemetery. "We could hide the formula at the Angel of Death's Motel," she declared dramatically.

"Yes!" I cried, laughing. I pedaled harder, passing Peggy in a renewed rush to get to the graveyard. The Angel of Death's Motel was the name we had given to a hill at the very back of the cemetery. A small stone mausoleum stood at the top, near a fence at the edge of the woods. We had decided this was a threatening place—the opposite, in fact, of The Angel of Love's Motel, which was located in another part of the cemetery. At The Angel of Love's Motel, a wide green field remained empty, so far, of the dead.

The most perilous things that occurred in our game happened at the Angel of Death's Motel. Sometimes, for example, we walked our bikes to the top of the steep hill and then rode them straight down, yelling, and screaming, and praying we'd make it to the bottom alive. On other days, we left our bikes at the top and lay down in the grass and leaves, our legs straight out and our arms above our heads. Then we rolled down the hill, laughing and shouting all the way, trying not to hit any gravestones. Movie-Man would never guess we would hide the formula in such a dangerous place.

Suddenly, metal screeched against metal as Peggy braked hard behind me. I heard her bike skid on the gravel on the shoulder of the road. I looked over my shoulder and saw that she had stopped and was climbing off her bike, which she laid in some weeds before bending over to look at something. I turned my bike in a wide arc in the middle of the road, which was still deserted, and rode back, stopping near Peggy. I hopped off my bike. "What is it?" I asked.

Peggy straightened up, her eyes still focused on the ground. I followed her gaze and saw what had caught her eye. Lying on its back, about a foot off the road, was a large blue jay. It had a tuft on its head, a ring of black feathers around its neck, and a light-gray breast. The bird wasn't moving. We looked at it in silence for a moment, and then Peggy stuck out her foot and nudged the small body gently with the toe of her sneaker. It still didn't move.

"He's dead," Peggy said matter-of-factly. She was pragmatic; I was over emotional. Tears sprang immediately to my eyes.

"Are you sure he's dead?" I asked shakily, taking a slow step backward, still staring at the bird.

"Yup, he's dead," she said. "We'd better bury him."

"How will we do that?" I asked. We hadn't planned for this. A bird wasn't supposed to die in our game. We had no box to put him in, no shovel. We couldn't pick up the bird and carry him anywhere, because neither of us had gloves. We had a vague notion that wild birds and animals could carry rabies or other diseases. Peggy didn't want to roll the bird farther into the weeds with a stick, because she thought that might damage him. We considered leaving him where he was and returning the next day with a shovel, but I was nervous that we might not find him again, or even worse, we might find only part of him.

I remembered some tissues that were stuffed in my jacket pocket. "Why don't we wrap him in these?" I asked, pulling out the crumpled tissues and showing them to Peggy.

Just when we had agreed on this plan, we heard an engine revving up as a car approached the top of the hill out of sight. "Car!" I yelled, and we dashed behind a large tree, leaving our bikes lying by the side of the road. We plastered ourselves against the trunk, breathing hard, and waited until the car had passed.

"That was close," Peggy said, still leaning against the tree and peeking slowly around it.

I nodded. "It might have been Movie-Man. Do you think he saw the bikes?"

"Well, let's just hope he was going too fast to notice," she said. "We have to bury this bird, and we have to bury him now. Maybe Movie-Man is after him."

We knelt down together next to the tree and started tearing into the ground with our bare hands, shoving dirt and old leaves to the side. A hole began to appear and then deepen. While we worked, I suggested that we give the bird a name.

"Why don't we call him B.B., for Blue Bird?" I asked.

"Well, he's a blue jay, but B.B. is just fine," Peggy said.

We kept digging, clawing at the ground and shoveling out the dirt with cupped hands. When the hole was finally big enough for B.B., we stood and brushed the soil and leaves off our pants, smearing more dirt on them in the process. I handed the tissues to Peggy. She walked over to B.B., bent down, and picked up the stiff body, wrapping it gently in the tissues before carrying it back to the tree. Then she laid the bird on its back in the center of the hole. We could still see its head. I looked hard into the round, black eyes, hoping to see something besides nothing, something different from death. I didn't see anger or fear in their depths. The eyes simply stared up toward the sky, above an open beak, as if B.B. had been stopped in the middle of something.

Peggy and I stood beside the makeshift grave and looked at the blue jay. "It seems so sad to cover him up," I said. Tears threatened again, and my throat tightened.

"We have to," Peggy said. "We have no choice. But we could give him a ceremony first." She thought for a moment before adding, "God, please watch over B.B. Take him up to heaven. He was a very good bird, and we loved him."

I tried to think of a prayer, and one that I knew in Hebrew popped into my head. I was pretty sure you were supposed to light candles when you said it, but I said it anyway. "*Baruch atah Adonai eloheinu melech haolum, asher kidishanu bemitzvotav vitzivanu lahadlich ner shel*...the funeral of B.B."

We stood silently, looking down at the bird, and another minute passed. I didn't think I could do it; it felt so wrong to cover that beautiful, bright blue bird with plain old dirt. *All he wanted was to live*, I thought, *all he wanted was to see the sky. Maybe he still could see the sky*. But Peggy said, "It's time."

We squatted back down, and I followed her lead, scooping

some of the dirt we'd dug out of the earth into my hands and slowly covering the bird.

We avoided his head until the very end. "Good-bye, B.B.," I whispered, the tears spilling out of my eyes now and onto the makeshift grave. "Good-bye, little friend."

There was nothing else to do. We each poured one final handful of dirt over the bird's head, and then B.B. was gone.

Peggy said, "Okay, we have work to do."

I took a deep breath, stood up, and followed her back to the edge of the road. We climbed onto our bikes and started pedaling again toward the cemetery. I glanced back just once, and then, in the way a child knows how, I let B.B. go.

Blue jays, with their bold blue plumage, white-gray breasts, tufted heads, piercing black eyes, and pointed beaks, rule the woods and backyards of the northeast. Like uniformed police, they take command of smaller birds; when I see them, I almost expect them to be carrying tiny nightsticks.

Blue jays guard their territory, taking advantage of their relatively large size to drive smaller species away from bird feeders. Occasionally they raid unsuspecting nests. Some bird lovers frown on such behavior and consider blue jays pests. Although I usually root for the underdog, I don't begrudge blue jays their aggressive nature. I can't blame a creature that lives its life the way it was meant to live.

The oldest wild blue jay studied by researchers, according to the University of Michigan Museum of Zoology, lived to be seventeen and a half years old. One captive female lived for twenty-six years and three months. *Do blue jays comprehend life and death?* I wonder. They are here, then gone, in a matter of years. Knowing this makes me sad. But is it any different for us?

Dr. Steven D. Farmer, the author of *Animal Spirit Guides*, is a shamanic practitioner with more than thirty years of experience as a healer and teacher. He resides in California, and has written several books about animals and appeared on both radio and television programs. He says that if a blue jay shows up in your path, it could signify a number of things. One message it brings might be this: "Whatever the situation that has triggered some fear, attack it boldly and courageously."

I stared in shock, through the rain dripping off my hood, at the bird standing on my boot. Had a wild blue jay just hopped onto my foot? I tried to collect my thoughts. This was getting ridiculous, I told myself. Wild birds don't stand around on the ground in the rain. They don't hop along paved pathways. They don't pause before crossing the road or move over in the middle of pedestrian crosswalks to let you pass by, and they certainly don't turn around and hop back toward you once you've crossed. But more than anything else, wild birds do not jump onto your foot.

Was this creature just a wild bird, then? I thought about my mother-in-law. This couldn't be her spirit, could it, returning to tell me something or to ask me to take care of her son? Maybe she was reprimanding me for abandoning her. After all, I was here on this campus walking to class, going on with my life when she could no longer live hers. Judith's reincarnation would be an obvious answer, a convenient way to explain what was happening. It would comfort me to think that her death had not been the end. But I knew, in my gut, that this bird was not Judith. Nothing about this experience felt like her. This experience felt like me.

"You have to go," I told the blue jay, my voice firm now. The jay stood on my boot and stared up at me. No other cars had driven by, no other students had walked this way. There was just this bird and me, alone in the cold, wet rain, surrounded by thick, dark trees, on a road that disappeared into nothing in both directions. "Please," I said, "you have to fly away."

The blue jay cocked its head slightly to the right, and I heard something—the engine of an approaching car. The white flash of headlights hit the corner of my eye.

That was it. I would have to reach down and pick up this bird so that we could both get out of this road. The jay was obviously hurt; it needed my help. It was my job to fix this. I would miss my class, I would miss dinner, I would miss out; but I would find a veterinarian and save this bird.

I leaned down to pick up the blue jay. But just as I did, the bird slowly lifted its wings. I froze in place, half bent over. The jay stretched its wings outward as if to drain off the rain and then, with barely a jump, flew off. Its flight was unhurried; I straightened up and watched as the bird disappeared between the trees in what seemed like slow motion, a fleck of vivid blue that got smaller and smaller before dissolving into the gray mist.

For some people a blue jay is just a blue jay, and death is just death. *I* am not so sure.

For twenty-two months I watched Judith die. I realize now that when it was over I stopped living, because in living there is so much to lose. A car can come barreling from any direction and hit us; it doesn't matter how careful we are. I have spent my life rescuing animals, birds, and even people, trying to spare them—and myself—from what I fear is the truth. I see that now. To prevent suffering has always been my purpose, but it has also been my only solace.

A blue jay came to me on a road in the rain in my forty-seventh year. The bird told me this: "You think you must save me, but I do not need to be saved. You cannot control these things. You cannot meet death face-to-face. You held Judith's gaze until she turned away. Now let her go. Let yourself go. Create meaning. Play. Because you can't change the rain on a January day."

# CHAPTER THIRTEEN

## Barred

It's the heart of winter in the northeast, and two feet of snow blanket the hills and fields that surround my parents' farmhouse in upstate New York. Jean-Paul and I are visiting from Boston, and we can't resist the call of the woods. We pull on ski jackets, snow pants, and well-worn boots. Once outside, we crunch across the snow that plows have packed down on the road. The frigid air pricks at our faces as we retrieve aluminum snowshoes from our Subaru Outback and strap them onto our boots. We clamber over a four-foot snow mound and survey the front field, which is a frozen, untainted white. I glance at Jean-Paul, and although his pale eyes are hidden behind dark sunglasses, I can see he is delighted. He lifts his right leg and shakes snow from his snowshoe, and soon we are moving forward side by side. We are two warm bodies exhaling wisps of white clouds, bound together by the splendor of the moment. I was alone for years before I met Jean-Paul, and during that time I felt isolated from the world. Now that I am with him I relish his companionship and am grateful for shared days such as this.

Our snowshoes prevent us from sinking too deep into the snow. We raise our legs high, swing them forward and down, rock back and forth like ski-jacket-clad zombies. The trees in their coats of ice glitter at the edge of the far field, tempting us on toward the woods. We pass the weather-beaten walls of the old hay barn, which leans to one side like the head of a sleepy student perilously close to collapsing onto his desk. Recently my father hired someone to paint the barn's metal roof, but now it is caked with a layer of snow.

My parents had purchased this property long after it ceased operating as a working farm. After we'd moved here from the city when I was six, a farmer from across the valley continued to harvest hay from these fields. He stored it in the barn, and during the long, cold winters he used it to feed his horses and cows. The farmer is long gone now, and over the years the barn has fallen into disrepair. All I can see when I glance through an open back entrance is an archaic green Ski-Doo. We used to ride it joyfully over these fields, jumping over the dens dug by woodchucks. Now the machine rusts alone in a corner. I quickly look away.

A narrow path leads us past the barn and through an old apple orchard, where a small, spring-fed pond lies in the middle of the trees. Sparkling branches hang over the frozen pond, which hides beneath layers of snow and ice. The bullfrogs are silent; their husky croaks will echo through the long summer nights after they emerge from hibernation in the spring. A tree felled by a beaver rests on the ice, but no beaver dam is in evidence. I take a step forward, but Jean-Paul cautions me not to get too close. We regard the pond from a safe distance for a while.

The skin on my face is turning red with cold, and my fingers feel stiff inside my gloves. I pull my arms closer to my sides, and Jean-Paul, sensing my discomfort, turns to leave. We tramp back through the trees and circle around the pond, making our way toward the far field. Jean-Paul—taller and heavier than I—trudges rapidly ahead, invigorated by the open sky and crisp air. Snow flicks off the edges of his snowshoes.

My heart beats harder in my chest, and I struggle in an effort to keep up.

Someone has laid a wooden plank across the narrow creek that drains water from the back of the pond. The creek bubbles even in winter. Ralph, a neighbor who helps my father with the upkeep of the land, probably left the plank behind. Jean-Paul crosses the creek and turns back toward me, extending a gloved hand. I can manage myself, but I accept the assistance.

We trek on determinedly, closing in on the woods with every step. The field slopes gently upward, and we stop at one point to turn around and enjoy the view. The hills are stark in winter, the color of dirty slate, and they loom large against the blue sky. It feels as if we have been transported into a classic Russian novel, and our goal is to cross this frozen wasteland in search of some critical, universal truth.

We resume our march forward and, finally, after a few minutes, reach the far edge of the field. Bare maples, oaks, and slim, white birches surround us as we enter the woods. The occasional pine tree provides a shock of green. I stop, look up, and glimpse patches of pale sky through an endless tangle of branches. The trees are like frozen ballerinas on silent music boxes, their arms stretched outward, fingers pointing forever toward the sky.

The air is frigid. No birds call. No traffic sounds from the New York Thruway—which passes through the valley a mile from here—penetrate the thick wall of trees. The sunshine splinters into fragments as it filters toward the forest floor. Jean-Paul forges deeper into the woods, snowshoes thumping. I choose to stay here, to enjoy the stillness once Jean-Paul is out of earshot. A few weeks from now the snow will be gone. Buds will appear and expand into leaves, and sap will start flowing through the maples. The groundhogs will awaken and emerge from their dens. Deer, now hidden somewhere deep in the woods, will bear fawns who will wander toward the field.

Migrating birds will return, filling the woods with the trill of their songs. Crickets will sing with their wings. I feel at one with all this, and a surge of joy passes through me.

Jean-Paul calls out; the sound pierces my reverie. For a second I think he is crying for help. I look around and hear him again, calling my name. I turn toward the sound and peer between the tree trunks past his tracks in the snow. I see nothing. He calls again, and his words race over the snow.

"I see an owl; I am looking right at him!" he says. I plunge forward through the snow, following his tracks, tramping as quickly as I can toward the sound of his voice. Within moments I see Jean-Paul standing among the trees. When I reach him, he is staring up at the forest canopy. I follow his gaze and search among the branches, but I don't see the owl.

"It flew away," Jean-Paul says, smiling dreamily, his dark sunglasses reflecting the bright sun. "It was so beautiful. It was white, maybe thirty feet away. Up there, on that branch." He points to a spot above us.

I examine the branch and notice an area where the snow has been disturbed. I have never seen an owl in the wild. I try to swallow the disappointment lodged in my throat.

"It looked right at me, right at me!" Jean-Paul says. "We stared at each other for at least thirty seconds! But then it flew away, over there." He points again, this time deeper into the woods. He sees the regret on my face now and wants to share the sighting with me. I scan the trees and catch, just for a second, in the periphery of my vision, what appears to be a large bird winging away. But by the time I turn to look, the bird is gone.

"It flew this way," Jean-Paul says, not wanting to give up, and we head farther into the woods, toward the edge of my parents' property. But even as I drag my snowshoes through the deepening snow, I know that we won't find the owl. If it did fly this way, Jean-Paul's excited shouts and our heavy, awkward steps will have frightened it off by now.

We search for maybe ten minutes but never find the owl. Jean-Paul talks excitedly about his encounter, and I battle disappointment. I feel selfish. I'm surprised that it seems so important that I didn't see the owl. Why can't I just be happy that Jean-Paul did?

Eventually he falls silent, and we make our way back to the house.

We remove our snowshoes and load them back into the car. A burst of cold air pursues me through the front door of the house. My mother is washing dishes in the kitchen, and as I pull off my boots and shrug off my jacket, I tell her that Jean-Paul saw an owl.

My mother enjoys birdwatching and is immediately interested. Jean-Paul enters the hallway, twisting his head side to side to shake the snow from his hair. My mother asks him about the owl, and he shares all the details as he throws his coat over a hook on the wall.

"Did you see it?" my mother asks me.

"No," I say. "But the woods were beautiful," I add, determined to retrieve something from the loss.

We discuss the sighting, and my mother guesses that the bird Jean-Paul saw was a barred owl, which is common in the area. She removes a book titled *Birds of New York* from a drawer and hands it to me. I turn to the index and begin searching for the listing.

My mother asks if we'd like some hot coffee, and I nod my head, still scanning the index. Jean-Paul joins us in the kitchen, rubbing his hands together to warm them after the cold. "Your face is bright red!" my mother tells him. He laughs with pleasure, as if the redness of his skin adds to his adventure. Then he approaches with curiosity and looks over my shoulder, and a tug of affection overtakes my discontent.

I find the barred owl listed in the index and flip to the

middle of the book. A stunning bird, white with brown markings, stares up at me from the page. And in that moment, standing side by side with my husband looking at the picture of the owl I did not see, I realize my mistake. No life is fully shared. Loneliness is always waiting, like the water beneath the wooden plank that Ralph placed over the creek. Togetherness is just a fortress we build against it. And that's why, when Jean-Paul extended his hand, I took it.

# CHAPTER FOURTEEN

# Sugarloaf

July 30: midday, midsummer, midlife. Midway through the first of three summers I will spend alone while Jean-Paul pursues a PhD at Smith College. I am seated at a picnic table on the lawn between two buildings at Sugarloaf Estates, an apartment complex in Sunderland, Massachusetts. Don't let the name fool you; there are no sweet, fertile fields or manor houses here. Sugarloaf Estates is an uninspired, worn-out apartment complex built next to a two-lane country road. Jean-Paul is subletting an apartment on the third floor of one of the buildings near the entrance. I arrived here yesterday after driving across the state to escape the heat, humidity, and noise of a Boston summer. I *had* to get out, at least for the weekend. But it disappoints me to realize that I don't feel much better as I sit at this picnic table 108 miles from all that. No matter how many miles I put on that car, I can't escape the workings of my mind.

The bench attached to the picnic table feels rough beneath my legs. The table itself is badly warped; it's hard to say when it might have been new. The buildings here strike me as barrack-like: long, rectangular, redbrick. The asphalt parking lots are faded and cracked, and the lawns, though green, are overgrown. I am clearly taking note of the objects that match my mood;

otherwise I would comment on the hint of woods beyond the apartments or the pine tree next to the picnic table, with its thick branches blanketed in green. I would listen with more delight to the short, swift chirps of the sparrows I cannot see. It is Saturday. I am not working. I should feel easy, lively, full of breath, free. Instead I feel pinched, as craggy as the chain-link fence that surrounds a small swimming pool nearby. It reminds me of the rusty fences in front of some of the houses in our neighborhood; they lend a junkyard character to the streets. I have long wished that somehow, in the middle of the night, an arm of God or the universe would sweep through the town and take those ugly fences away.

Jean-Paul has been frustrated by my downbeat attitude about both our neighborhood and our house. I wonder, when examining my dissatisfaction, at what some might call a sense of entitlement. But perhaps it is acceptable to confess my true self and admit that I have dreams of a different life, one spent, perhaps, in a home I could love, with gleaming hardwood floors and a fenced-in back porch overlooking a spacious garden at the edge of the woods.

When I moved into our house before we were married, during the period when Jean-Paul was renting it from his mother, we stripped the yellowed wallpaper that was peeling off the walls, hired a handyman to install new Sheetrock, and coated the entire interior with fresh paint. I laid updated linoleum over the scratched, dirty floors in the kitchen and the bathroom. The sons of the previous owners had scrawled graffiti inside the upstairs closet doors—I discovered a swastika on one—and it took extra coats of paint to conceal the damage. When we found live bullets on the floor of one of the closets, we turned them over to the police.

Even after these improvements, the house still needed a lot of work, but we had done all we could afford to at the time. I told Jean-Paul I could see myself living in the house for maybe five years. A year later, Jean-Paul and I got engaged. Four months after that his mother's brain cancer was discovered, and she asked us to take the house off her hands.

The memory of the closing still haunts me. Judith was in a wheelchair by then, confined within the walls of her small Cambridge house. We sat on the love seat in her living room, next to the lawyer she'd hired who had pulled up a chair. A layer of dust, loose papers, torn envelopes, and dirty dishes covered every surface in the room. The lawyer laid the closing documents on top of the cluttered coffee table. Judith, in her wheelchair on the opposite side of the table, picked up the documents, scanned them one by one, and then started screaming.

"I'm getting cheated! I'm getting cheated!" she cried as Jean-Paul and the lawyer tried to calm her, explaining that everything had been handled exactly as she'd requested.

Finally, her eyes swollen and red, tears streaming down her cheeks, Judith leaned forward and signed the papers. Her hands shook as she scratched out her name. When she finished, she wheeled herself from the room and into her kitchen. Jean-Paul and I sat side by side, shocked and mortified, while the lawyer gathered up the papers. He shook our hands quickly, said "Congratulations on your new home," and left.

This May we hit the five-year mark I had set for living in the house. In June I stood at the front door, offering a halfhearted wave as Jean-Paul pulled out of the driveway and headed west. I watched his car disappear around the corner, then stepped back into the house and closed the door.

I have never felt more abandoned. I have never felt more stuck.

I look up from the picnic table and rest my eyes on the view beyond Sugarloaf Estates. The long, flat fields of a working farm lie just across the road from the apartment complex. Neat rows of corn stretch toward a horizon marked by rolling hills and a pale-blue sky. I read somewhere that New England is the only region of the United States where the forests have reclaimed lost ground. The trees in Massachusetts are more stubborn, apparently, than the Colonial settlers who established their homesteads here. Evidence of the early farmers still endures, however, and has become a part of the New England landscape. Stone walls snake through the woods, reminders of original farm boundaries. Barns that once housed animals or stored bales of hay stand, like nervous children, near white wooden farmhouses. Some of the barns are faded and weathered, leaning heavily from neglect next to overgrown pastures. Others are well cared for, freshly painted and still in use. Sheep, cows, and goats still graze near fields that produce corn or hay. The odor of manure drifts off small dairy farms, and the roads wind past pumpkin patches and apple orchards.

But modern life intrudes on what were once purely bucolic scenes. Small strip malls offer doughnuts, pizza, groceries, and gasoline along the roads. Amherst and Northampton, built up over the years around the local college campuses, serve as the cultural centers of the region. Their main streets boast bookstores, restaurants, bars, and coffee shops. Students in sandals and jeans or peasant skirts carry cell phones and backpacks and roam up and down the streets.

Sunderland is somewhat removed from all that. It takes twenty minutes to drive from Sugarloaf Estates to either Amherst or Northampton. Here everything is still about the land and the trees, the sun and the crops. Here bees buzz around the yards and flowers, sparrows and chickadees flit among the trees, red-tailed hawks circle in the sky above the fields.

When I was growing up, our corner of upstate New York offered a similar quiet serenity, although our farmhouse was nestled in the hills. The landscape here is more open, yet it stirs a familiar yearning. Sometimes I miss the natural world so much my gut actually tightens in pain. Now, as I gaze at the land that stretches west across the road, I feel the tension in my shoulders slowly ease.

The sky is calm. The air is warm but bearable. Sugarloaf Estates appears to be largely deserted. The parking lots are empty, and the only person in view is a man who has fallen asleep on a lounge chair beside the pool. His hands are clasped loosely on his lap. It occurs to me that I am never as relaxed as he appears. Lately, I have blamed Jean-Paul's decision to return to graduate school for the frustration I feel as I drift through the tedium of a lonely summer in the city. I wake up, work at my desk, clean the house, work some more, gaze at the backyard through the kitchen window, stare at the street from our front door. I fall asleep next to an unread book in the afternoon, wake up, and return to my desk.

I should admit I was struggling before Jean-Paul left. In fact, even before he entered my life. Over the years a few doctors have diagnosed generalized anxiety. They have prescribed talk therapy and pills. I've tried both. But in the end two things always remain the same: the world as it exists, and me. I was always fidgety, even as a child. I remember lying in my room staring at the ceiling, feeling as if my mind was bouncing off the walls. Perhaps my father's decision to continue working in the city after we moved north instilled a kind of instability, a sense that there was another world out there, that our family was never fully here nor there and that no place was ever quite home.

Before Jean-Paul left for Sugarloaf Estates, a friend suggested I dedicate the next few months to my creative work. I could designate a special space in the house for my writing and even prepare meals in advance to heat up throughout the week. It would be like attending my own personal writing retreat, she said. My paid freelance work would have to get done, but I could set aside a few hours each morning for that and consider the rest of the day my own. Rather than frame the summer as something to endure, I could envision it as a rare opportunity.

I have tried, but now that summer is half over I have to admit my efforts to be creative have fallen flat. After I finish my paying work, I find things to do around the house. I vacuum or mop. I refill the cats' water bowl. I sprinkle the flowers I planted along the front walkway in the spring. I drive to the bank to deposit any checks that have arrived in the mail and buy groceries at the supermarket before I head home. I stop at the gas station and fill the car with gas. When I get home, I do the bookkeeping and worry over our bank account. I wander around the town in circles—house to bank, to supermarket, to house—living as I have always lived, holding the carrot of happiness just beyond reach in front of my own face.

I pause from my typing, look up from my laptop, and stare at the redbrick buildings that combine to create Sugarloaf Estates. In one of those buildings Jean-Paul is working amid scattered piles of papers. The dishes from his last meal still sit in the kitchen sink. The mattress on the floor of his bedroom is covered by a blanket he tossed over it carelessly this morning. His bathroom is dirty, and his laundry is piling up on the floor. He reads and writes in the middle of all that. Yet his mind wanders freely, more liberated than mine has ever been.

I sit quietly for a while, and eventually, because there is nothing else to do, I find myself listening to the birds that I have been only hearing until now. Their twitters, chirps, and peeps surround me like a canopy of ringing bells. I am reminded of the voice of R2-D2, one of the droids in *Star Wars*. I wonder, for the first time, if birdsongs were the inspiration for the robot's voice. It hits me suddenly that a sound engineer created that unmistakable voice. I am fascinated by the possibility that a human imagination might have made such a leap and transformed the sound of birdsongs into a voice beloved by millions.

What bars such a discovery from my own restless mind? Is it really the crumbling walls of our run-down, old house?

A young man walks by wearing jeans and a t-shirt. He is leading a trim, athletic boxer on a canvas leash. The dog wriggles with pleasure as it trots by the man's side, enjoying the simple experience of spending time outdoors. Suddenly the dog dips its head and grabs a piece of the leash in its mouth before sauntering happily on. I consider the animal's willingness—even joy—at taking part in its own captivity. But then it occurs to me that the dog might not see things that way. Perhaps the leash, in the dog's mind, is not an imprisoning thing. It is the object that makes it possible to be outside.

I look again at Sugarloaf Estates. It is an apartment complex built next to a two-lane country road in Sunderland, Massachusetts—nothing less and nothing more. These buildings house young families who live in the area for a few years or college students who arrive in packed cars in the fall and leave the following spring. One of the buildings, near the entrance, houses my husband, who is studying at Smith College this summer.

But these redbrick walls do not contain me. Just there, across the road, the fields breathe with life. Hawks circle high above the trees. In the distance, the hills are splashed against the sky. And there is nothing, absolutely nothing, to stop me from standing up and walking across that road.

# CHAPTER FIFTEEN

# Waiting for the Hurricane

The turquoise sea rolls back and forth, as restless as a tiger pacing the walls of a cage. The moon, pale yet luminous, takes a last, tender look as it gives way to the sun. The peeping of the tree frogs fades with the darkness, and the birds begin their morning songs. It is an in-between moment, not night, not day. Shading my eyes, I scan the horizon. There is no visible sign, apart from the agitated waves, that a category four hurricane is headed toward Bermuda.

Last night, before Jean-Paul and I went to bed, I switched on the television in our hotel room. I browsed through the stations—CNN International, a network from Miami, the Africa Channel—until I found the emergency weather alerts. Rudimentary text ran across a plain screen. Hurricane Danielle, according to the latest update, was expected to swerve east before morning. Bermuda would likely be spared a direct hit, although rain, strong winds, and riptides were possible. Small-craft warnings were in effect. I should have felt relieved. TV meteorologists had been pointing excitedly at Doppler images of the Atlantic for a week before our trip, focusing their attention on a whirling mass of wind that was growing in size and moving steadily northwest. Danielle, they declared, would likely hit Bermuda, arriving within a day of when we were scheduled to land on what we had hoped would be an island paradise.

Jean-Paul, thankfully, rarely watches the news. He is a nervous flier and I didn't want to add the specter of a hurricane to his fears. When we talked about the trip, I avoided any mention of the approaching storm. I just told him to pack shirts with collars for the formal restaurants, and to pour shampoo and conditioner into containers we could pack in our carry-on luggage. We agreed that I didn't need to bring my own snorkeling gear, because we could rent what we needed at the Pompano Beach Club. I never considered canceling our plans. The idea of this escape had carried me through a difficult summer. I couldn't let the dream go now. Besides, I told myself, the hurricane might only glance Bermuda—tip its hat, so to speak, and move on.

In the end, the flight was uneventful. We landed safely at L. F. Wade International Airport and took a prearranged shuttle van to the Pompano. That was Thursday, the day before yesterday. For the next twenty-four hours Bermuda remained on alert. By Friday, however, word was getting around that Danielle might not make landfall. Most tourists, I was sure, breathed a sigh of relief. My own reaction surprised me.

I felt disappointed.

This morning, trying to move quietly so I wouldn't wake Jean-Paul, I slipped between the floor-length curtains and slid open the glass doors to the balcony. Heat and humidity enveloped me as I stepped outside the air-conditioned room. I shut the doors and settled onto a lounge chair with a small table next to it. Then I placed my notebook and pen on my lap, and surveyed the scene in front of me.

The pink and white buildings of the Pompano Beach Club sit on terraces forged out of the rocky coastline. Our building, located near the highest point,  provided a stunning view of the sea. Stone staircases connect the upper terraces to the main building below, allowing access to a small beach at the edge of the water. I couldn't see the beach from our balcony, but the sea stretched toward the horizon like an endless, turquoise bed-sheet, fluttering in the wind.

I take a deep breath, and warm air fills my lungs. I try to absorb the fact that after envisioning this getaway for so many weeks, I am actually here. I remember writing to the owner of the Pompano in July and telling him I was hoping for a balcony with an ocean view. He responded right away, promising to handpick our room. Now I am sitting on that balcony and feel an intense need to experience this place, to notice everything around me. I grasp at the sights, the scents, the sounds; but they flutter around me like butterflies, impossible to catch. I am keenly aware that in just two days Bermuda will be nothing but a memory.

While Jean-Paul wrote research papers in Northampton this summer, I had stayed home in Boston. I worked from my home office and struggled to pay the bills. I fed our three cats, cleaned their litter boxes, and brushed their thick summer coats. I chatted with neighbors about the unusually wet spring and planted orange marigolds around the edges of the back deck, and purple and pink petunias along the cracked cement walkway that leads from our front door to the street.

Friends had worried that I would be lonely, and called now and then to invite me to lunch. But it wasn't loneliness that troubled me as the days wore on. It was a haunting feeling that the future I had envisioned as a child might never come to pass. I wandered through the rooms of our house, trying to figure out why what I had wasn't enough. I picked up a framed photograph of Jean-Paul and me smiling, and looked at it for a while. I petted a cat sleeping in the sun near a window. I ran my fingers across the bindings of the books lining the shelves in my writing room. Outside, sitting at the table on our back deck, I watched a cardinal as it issued staccato chirps from a branch of the crabapple tree. It flew off, leaving me with an emptiness as real as hunger pangs.

I knew I had been waiting for as long as I could remember for something that I could not name in words. And although I couldn't identify this thing, I was beginning to suspect that it might never arrive.

Leaning against the back of the lounge chair, I stare out to sea and examine the horizon, then inspect the landscape around me. Beneath the balcony, a pathway winds through a carefully tended garden. The grass is an emerald green. A short, thick tree squats near the stone staircase. It looks like an oversize pineapple stuck halfway in the ground. The tree's long leaves sway in the breeze, reminding me of the tentacles of an octopus. Birds chatter, and although I can't see them, I imagine them hiding among the trees and flitting between the manicured hedges. The idea of the birds makes me happy. I take another breath.

I have always relished quiet, but even as I enjoy the serenity of this moment, a switch seems to flip in my head. I think about the hurricane and wonder if the breeze is stronger than usual, if the waves will become more dramatic. I remember how smooth the sea looked yesterday and am curious about how rough it might get.

Yesterday morning, the woman at the front desk gave us directions to the food market, then raised her eyebrows when we turned down a ride. We insisted on walking, an option not considered by most hotel guests. By 9 AM the temperature had reached the mid-80s, and the humidity was already oppressive. The driveway from the main building to the road is long and hilly. It passes several houses hidden at the top of small hills and cuts through one end of the Pompano's large golf course. When it finally meets the main road, the market is about 600 yards to the left.

Still, we wanted to immerse ourselves in the tropical feel

of the island, to see the thick, green loquat trees, the tall date palms, and the exotic Surinam cherry trees up close. So we walked. The air was heavy with the fragrance of bougainvillea, amaryllis, and hibiscus blossoms. By the time we reached the main road, our faces were red from the sun, and our t-shirts and shorts were damp with sweat. We turned toward the market and then walked past it, deciding to pick up groceries on the way back to the hotel. A short while later, we came to a bridge that Bermudians claim is the smallest drawbridge in the world and crossed over it onto Somerset Island.

Hugging the side of the narrow road, often without the benefit of a sidewalk, we walked past houses painted pastel colors: blue, pink, yellow, and green. Many of the homes had tidy English gardens accented with flowers. Between the neighborhoods, crops grew in small fields. We hugged a stone wall on one steep hill, hoping the buses that thundered past wouldn't hit us. When we arrived at a fork leading to a paved pathway on the right, Jean-Paul suggested we leave the road.

"This will get us away from the cars," he said. His pale skin was showing signs of sunburn. Jean-Paul has blue eyes and light hair, and his complexion isn't ideal for spending time in the sun. I have dark eyes and hair, and my skin rarely burns.

"Do you think we should start back?" I asked, peering as far as I could down the lane. I was thinking about the distance we had walked, the glare of the sun, and how long it would take us to get back to the hotel.

"I'm enjoying this," Jean-Paul said, unconcerned about all that. "Let's walk a little farther."

The path led toward the towering wall of an old fort. A large mangrove tree stood at the top of the wall, and cascading down the side was an astonishing tangle of mangrove tree roots. A few feet past the tree, on the other side of the path, an old staircase led through the grass and down a small hill. We followed the stairs to the edge of a wide body of water, which

I later found out is called the Great Sound.

The unfathomably clear inlet seemed to sparkle in the sun. We stood quietly for a while, staring across the sound to the opposite shore.

"I can't believe we found this spot by accident, and have it all to ourselves," I said.

Jean-Paul nodded, smiling.

Three hours after we left the Pompano, we returned carrying soda water, a bottle of vodka, and snacks for the room. Our faces and clothes were dripping with sweat. Blisters had formed under the straps of my sandals.

We were ready for a swim in the sea.

When we'd checked in at the Pompano on our first day in Bermuda, the staff informed us that at low tide the ocean is shallow all the way to the reef. Professional snorkeling expeditions head to the reef daily, although some visitors paddle out on rented watercraft, which they tie to the buoys while they snorkel. To avoid the cost of a kayak or paddleboat, we rented masks, snorkels, and flippers, and set out to swim the quarter mile to the reef.

It was afternoon, however, high tide, and the sea was soon deeper than we expected. The water was warm and salty on our skin, and the sun was hot on our backs. On the ocean floor, the white sand seemed to dance in the scattered sunlight. Jean-Paul and I are both strong swimmers, and we progressed at a relaxed pace, propelling ourselves forward with slow, even kicks. The only sound we could hear was the splashing of our flippers moving in and out of the water. The setting was idyllic, but as the water got deeper, I became more and more nervous, even though the scene beneath us didn't change. My stomach felt tighter, and my breathing quickened. The closer we got to the looming shadow of the reef, the more anxious I became. Intellectually, I knew there was no real danger; sharks aren't often seen off the coast of Bermuda, and a shark attack hadn't been reported in years. Still, I have had a phobia about sharks ever since I saw *Jaws* as a child, and as we approached the reef, I began to think I might panic. I signaled Jean-Paul, pointing back toward the shore. He nodded and emitted a garbled "Okay" through his snorkel. We turned and headed back to the beach.

This morning, I regret that decision to turn around. I wanted to explore the reef; I am sure I would have enjoyed seeing the tropical fish. I have snorkeled in the ocean before, although usually under the supervision of professional guides. Now, with the water kicked up by the hurricane, I suspect I won't get another chance on this trip. Today's snorkeling expeditions will likely be suspended, along with the rental of small boats and equipment.

Thinking about my disappointment, I forget the joy of the swim.

Crests of white foam are beginning to signal rough conditions farther out at sea. The buoys near the reef are bouncing in the waves; and a square wooden raft, anchored to the seafloor a short distance from shore, is pitching up and down. I take another deep breath, feel my lungs expand, smell salt and flowers in the humid air. I look at the words I have been scratching in my notebook, and they stare back at me, ragged and uneven on the page.

Our room is located in a small, square cottage. The main building, below, houses the beach club's front desk and foyer, a small bar and lounge, two restaurants with large windows facing the sea, and a game room with a pool table and Ping-Pong table. From here I can see where the building opens to a large outdoor patio with a lima bean-shaped swimming pool. Tables with pink and white umbrellas surround the pool. The umbrellas are tied shut because of the early hour or maybe, I think, because of the impending hurricane.

Beyond the main building, large white clouds hang low

above the water. The only obvious sound, besides the calls of the invisible birds, is the monotonous hum of the HVAC as it cools the main building. Occasionally, I catch the slap of a wave as it crashes against the rocks.

A Kiskadee flycatcher, about ten inches long from the tip of its beak to the end of its tail, suddenly lands on the balcony railing. We stare at each other for a moment. A black stripe runs across the center of its white head, making it look like a robber wearing a mask. I am struck by the vividness of its yellow breast. I have never seen a Kiskadee flycatcher before. As I admire the bird, it turns toward the garden and lets loose a raucous call, like a trumpeter summoning a regiment. After a few more boisterous cries, the bird spreads its wings and takes off.

The pineapple-like tree dances a slow hula, and the breeze lifts the hair gently off my forehead and cheeks. For a moment I think about nothing.

Yesterday morning, the first time I sat out here, I spotted a school of gray fish in the water near the beach. They swam toward the shore, moving as one, reversed their direction, then reversed it again, the ultimate synchronized swimmers. Forward and backward, sometimes swirling in circles, the fish followed the gentle motion of the current. I reflected on the idea of rolling with the punches, moving without resistance to the ebbs and flows of life. But as I considered the thought, the fish leaped from the water and hung for a split second in the air. Their bodies, in formation, flashed silver in the sunlight before splashing back into the sea. It happened so fast I wasn't sure I had seen it. But a short time later they did it again.

For a second I am like the fish in midair, fully in the moment between what was and what will be. I get a glimpse of what it is like to exist wholly in the middle. But the moment passes, and the sensation slips away. It is replaced by a familiar watchfulness, and suddenly I understand. The danger is not the hurricane. The danger is the waiting.

# CHAPTER SIXTEEN

# The Hope

Achorus of birds nudged me awake. I lay still, eyes closed, as the chirps and whistles called and lulled. The sound was like water flowing in a brook set to music: peaceful, gentle, melodic, hopeful. A child dancing alone in a room. I opened my eyes and looked up at the ceiling. The only window was carved from the thick cement wall. Thin, white curtains were pulled to the side, but horizontal steel shutters blocked the morning light. I pushed the cotton sheet off my body (it had been too warm for a blanket) and stood on the mattress so I could push open the blinds. The birdsong swelled, and a shaft of bright sunlight streamed into the room, tilting slightly downward toward the door on the opposite wall. I would miss all this: the bed that filled most of the space in the small room, the walls Hagit and Ilan had recently painted white, the fractured outline of tall, slim, twelve-year-old Talia on the opposite side of the beveled glass door. It was April 2011, and the Passover week had just started. But in an hour Hagit, my second cousin, would drive me to Ben Gurion Airport, where I would board a twelve-hour flight to Newark. By dinnertime I would be back in Boston, far away from the Passover celebrations that were still taking place all over Israel, the home that for me will never be home.

Retrieving my iPhone from the small bedside table, I

activated the video function; and, standing on the bed again, I held the phone up near the window to record the sound of the birds greeting the morning amid the apartment buildings of Givataim, a small city bordering Tel Aviv. Hagit lived on the top floor of a four-story building, and the video would preserve the view of the pale-pink sky, the slanting rooftops beyond the corner of the next building, and the green tips of date palms and ficus trees. But what I wanted to record most was the sound of the birds, a reminder of the first morning I had ever spent in Israel.

It was 1985, and I was twenty-two and visiting Israel for the first time. At the beginning of my trip, I stayed south of Tel Aviv at a kibbutz called Kvutzat Shiller. An American friend whom I had known since childhood was living on the kibbutz at the time. He had moved to Israel at the age of eighteen, joined the army, and took a Hebrew name: Roee, the translation of his English name, Shepherd. Because Roee had no family in Israel, he had been "adopted" by the kibbutz, which served as his home base when he was on leave from the army. On my first morning in Israel, I stepped outside Roee's cottage, blinked in the morning sunlight, and felt the hot, damp air on my skin. And I heard for the first time that strident symphony of Israeli birdsong: tweets, chirps, and singsong calls that burst from the trees and held me instantly mesmerized. The sound rained down around me and at the same time floated up toward the sky. It's possible that the sound was heightened by other triggers to my senses: the bright morning light, the glimpse of fluttering wings among trees whose branches hung heavy with oranges, the fragrance of bright flowers I did not recognize and could not name, the heat that baked my arms and face. And I have no doubt that I was also overcome by emotion: after twenty-two years living as part of a minority in the United States, I was, for the first time, surrounded by people whose heritage and traditions I shared.

When my parents first traveled to Israel in the 1950s, before I was born, the northern hills of the Galil were fertile and lush, but the desert to the south was dry and barren, traversed mainly by rutty dirt roads. My father has often said that when they visited the southern tip of the country, the community of Eilat, on the shore of the Red Sea, consisted of only basic, rudimentary structures. Today Eilat has blossomed into a tourist destination that boasts beaches, an undersea aquarium, and world-class resorts. Drip agriculture and other developments have transformed areas of the Negev into thriving communities, the result of a decades-long effort to "turn the desert green."

When I was twenty-eight, I had lived in Israel for a year. Large expanses of barren land still separated the major cities. Bedouins still roamed the desert with their camels and slept in large tents, although generators provided electricity. Buses were the major form of transportation both within and between the largest cities. As far as access to most modern conveniences went, the country, overall, still trailed the United States. The few railways that existed were slow and overcrowded. Cable television was new and a novelty. Imported clothes and other products cost significantly more than they did in the United States. Home appliances were so expensive that the government granted special rights to new immigrants that enabled them to ship appliances to Israel from their home countries. I remember washing my clothes in the bathtub of the small flat I rented in a residential neighborhood of Jerusalem. I used a washboard to scrub any stains.

The Jerusalem I recalled was situated high in the hills an hour east of Tel Aviv. The climb up the roads that snaked toward the city inspired a breathtaking drama of arrival. Every building was constructed of Jerusalem stone, contributing to the tawny glow and ancient feel of the streets while rendering the views both glorious and picturesque. The celebrated

Old City seemed to stand apart, with the Dome of the Rock shining gold in the sun above the ancient battlements and old stone ramps that sloped up toward the fabled gates. I had always thought of Jerusalem as frozen in time and assumed that when I returned to the city, the streets would look familiar. But when Hagit's father, Shmuel, brought me there for a day in 2011, I was surprised; I recognized almost nothing. Jerusalem stone still reigned, but few of the streets or buildings looked familiar. Newly built tunnels accommodated a modern highway that led directly into the city, and the traffic was astonishing. A light-rail was in the process of being tested for commuters, and urban sprawl now surrounded the Old City. A trendy, expensive mall had been built just across the street, although to maintain the architectural cohesiveness of the city, the shops were incorporated into the facades of ancient buildings.

Only within the towering walls of the Old City was everything just as I remembered. Tourists crowded the narrow stone alleyways and picked through the souvenirs being sold in the busy Arab market. Long lines of the Christian faithful waited to enter the Church of the Holy Sepulcher. Jews from around the world prayed reverently at the Western Wall and squeezed handwritten notes into the cracks between its stones. But the Muslim holy site on the Temple Mount, the Dome of the Rock, was closed the day I was there. The site is maintained by a Muslim religious trust, a body under the auspices of the government of Jordan, and access by tourists was restricted.

Israel encompasses just 8,000 square miles; the country is 263 miles long from north to south, and 71 miles wide at its widest point and just 9 miles at its narrowest. Israel could fit into the state of Florida three times over, yet by 2011 the population had swelled to nearly eight million people. The country felt small and almost claustrophobic, partly due to the changing access to different areas. In the early 1990s I could visit parts of the West Bank that were now considered unsafe. In 1991 a friend drove me from Jerusalem to Bethlehem so I could witness the scene at Manger Square, albeit in a car fitted with bulletproof windows. In 2011 no one suggested the same short drive. After our day in Jerusalem, Shmuel drove me to a newly developed city called Modi'in to visit my first cousin Michele, who as an adult had moved to Israel from America. Our car had to pass through a security checkpoint on the highway. The highway itself had become a bone of contention because of certain areas where it passed through the West Bank. The land had been handed over to Palestinian control, but Israel needed the road it had built to link the Israeli cities. It is well known that such discord is born of decades of violence and conflicting religious and political views. But it is hard to imagine—unless you drive through the region—the challenges inherent in dividing such a small area between people who have profoundly contradictory claims.

During this visit, Islamic militants shot rockets into southern Israel from the Gaza Strip, hitting a school bus and killing a sixteen year-old Israeli boy. Israel retaliated with air strikes. Much of the world learned the news, if they heard it at all, through headlines mixed with other stories on the Internet or as a brief sound bite on an evening broadcast focused on more local events. But I sat around a television in Tel Aviv with Hagit, her husband, and her two children in the evenings to watch extended, detailed news reports and absorb whatever information was available. I experienced minor jolts of fear as I watched video of rockets landing in a city that was less than ninety minutes away by bus, but the fear was tempered by a trust in Israel's defense forces, which are among the best in the world. Every person in the room with me either had been in the Israeli army or would be one day; there was a sense that the army was family, and there was pride in the broadcasters' voices when they noted how many of the militants' rockets had been destroyed by Israel's new "Iron Dome" technology.

But the violence wasn't out of an R-rated movie; it was real. When Hagit answered her cell phone, speaking into it in rapid Hebrew, I understood that Anat, Hagit's sister, was visiting her mother-in-law in a city south of Tel Aviv called Ashkelon and that warning sirens had sounded in the streets. Anat was forced to retreat to a bomb shelter during the rocket fire along with her ten-year-old twin daughters. Both girls had cerebral palsy and were in wheelchairs. They remained in the shelter until the warning sirens stopped. Anat was letting Hagit know that everyone was all right.

"*Ha col beseder*," Hagit said when she got off the phone— everything is okay.

In Israel, everyone knows someone who has been touched by the latest conflict. Learning where and when the most recent rockets have fallen or the latest terrorist attacks have occurred might change your plans for travel the next day. Or you might shrug your shoulders, as many Israelis do, and go wherever you planned to go anyway.

There is another nation of human beings on the other side of this conflict. Of course the Palestinian people have as much right to live and prosper as the Israelis. But most of what I've read about Israel in the Western media has not matched my personal experience of the country's situation or accurately reflected the desire for peace that I have seen pulsing through the Israeli people.

What I lack is the hard shell that has developed around many Israelis as a result of the permanent state of vigilance in which they live. Their pain is masked by a steely determination to survive and succeed. It is true that in some cases the response to hatred is hatred, but most of the people I met were weary of the conflict and shared an underlying sadness that was vanquished, to an extent, by living life to the fullest. I once asked Hagit how it felt to know that her thirteen-year-old son, Matan, would one day be a soldier. During my visit, Matan spent most of his time visiting friends, teasing his sister, and avoiding his homework. Hagit sighed and said, "Every generation hopes that they will be the last to fight. But then it goes on. What can you do? You keep hoping, and you keep living."

For the most part, Israelis relish the small rewards of their complicated lives; they dote on their children, devour education, savor good food, wander the beaches, swim in the sea, and hike amid the canyons with a joy and appreciation rarely matched in other countries I have visited; and the country had certainly flourished over the last twenty years. Cement apartment buildings seemed to have cropped up everywhere, spreading over the landscape like vines. New cities had materialized between the cities I remembered. A modern train now breezed between Tel Aviv and Modi'in, and there were plans to extend the line into Jerusalem. Several tall buildings now dominated the Tel Aviv skyline, including the three buildings that formed the Azrieli Center and housed a large mall, corporate offices, and a Crowne Plaza hotel. Motorcycles sped along new, modern highways, weaving through long lines of traffic at rush hour. An electric car network was being tested in the central and northern parts of the country—the first one developed anywhere in the world. Cell phones were glued to the ears of practically every pedestrian on the street. At night, in Tel Aviv, the newly renovated seaport bustled with young people adorned in the latest global fashions. They prowled the boardwalk, sipped coffee at cafés, and waited to enter trendy nightclubs at roped-off entrances. In the city of Ra'anana, not far from Tel Aviv, my American cousin, Brynn, talked about the great deal she had recently gotten at a local store on a stylish pair of Italian shoes.

Even in Givataim—where Hagit has lived all her life—it seemed as if everything around us was in flux. Next door to

Hagit's building a construction crew was renovating one of the apartments. The echo of their hammers and the buzz of their chain saws disturbed the quiet of the early mornings. On the corner of the next block, a house had been torn down and was being replaced by a tall apartment building. The cars packed in tightly against the redbrick sidewalks now included not only small European models, but also a selection of large SUVs.

Only in remote areas of the Negev, or over the stretches of farmland of the northern Galil, or in the older residential neighborhoods of Jerusalem and Tel Aviv did I glimpse the Israel I remembered. During a day trip to the desert with Hagit's family, I relaxed into the familiar sights of the hard, tawny hills that stretched on for miles, the vast, empty skies, and the parched desert canyons that almost seemed to shimmer in the dry desert heat. As we drove toward Masada, my camera captured the silhouette of a Bedouin on a ridge above the road. He was leading a line of camels whose long, graceful necks dipping slightly with each step. The sun blazed hot on the back of my shirt as we climbed the Roman Ramp. At the top we wandered among the ruins of the ancient fortress and looked out over the Dead Sea at the pale horizon beyond the hills of Jordan.

At night, back in Givataim, the street below Hagit's apartment was empty and quiet. When I stood on the sidewalk and looked up into the darkness, I saw the frenetic flight of fruit bats as they darted between the branches of the ficus trees under the hazy glow of the streetlamps.

Hagit's mother is my mother's first cousin; our grandfathers were brothers born in Poland. Before World War II my grandfather Bernard escaped a political environment that was becoming increasingly hostile to the Jews by joining his older brother, Frank, in the United States. They waited for their third brother, Simcha, to follow, but at the last moment

Simcha boarded a boat that was headed for British-controlled Palestine. From that moment the family would be forever divided. Frank's and Bernard's children would be born in America, while Simcha's would be born in Israel.

I grew up in the United States without much extended family. My grandfather died of cancer when I was young, and his wife, my grandmother, passed away when I was sixteen. My father, who was born in Poland, survived the Holocaust and moved to America with his parents and three sisters, but I never knew his mother and father. They died of heart ailments before I was born. My father became estranged from his sisters for reasons that were never fully explained to me, and I have only vague memories of their children. The only extended family I truly knew during my youth was my mother's brother, his wife, and their three daughters. I was raised in a farmhouse in upstate New York while they lived in an apartment building in Coop City in the Bronx, not far from where my mother had spent her childhood. Of the three daughters, Michele now lives in Modi'in, Brynn lives north of Tel Aviv in a city called Ra'anana, and Shari, the oldest, has lived on a kibbutz near Eilat for almost thirty years. All of them are raising their children in Israel.

While many Americans describe their ethnic heritage by using references to countries of origin such as Irish, Italian, or Greek, I can only refer to a religion. I am Jewish. If asked to name my family's homeland, I am unsure what to say. Is it Poland or Russia, where my father and all my grandparents were born but where their communities were never integrated or accepted into the local culture? Do I call a country my family's homeland if any family members who didn't escape the place were rounded up, sent to concentration camps, and murdered? No.

Is our homeland Italy, where my maiden name was formed after an alliance between two families in the sixteenth century?

I have been mistaken for Italian more than once, but Italian culture doesn't match my family's culture, and the description doesn't seem to fit.

Is my homeland the United States, regardless of whether or not my father or any of my grandparents were born there? Do I attach myself to the country in which I was born like a child who clings to its mother? I don't know.

My relatives in Israel don't share my confusion; regardless of whether they were born in Israel or have moved there over the years, they wake up every morning in the place that has been their homeland since the time of a Biblical promise God made to Abraham. So whenever I am in Israel I search my body, my mind, and my heart for the certainty they feel. I wait patiently for it to overtake me. I sense the energy that courses through the streets and the people, and try to absorb it into my own skin. I let the sounds of the language enter empty crevices in my mind and give rise to images that are absent in English. I watch the waves of the Mediterranean lap against the shores as the sun sets behind the hotels in Tel Aviv. I am transfixed by the lights of the ancient port of Jaffa as they shine over the water at night. I breathe the hot, dry air into my lungs in the desert and feel the crunch of earth beneath my boots. I run my hands along the smooth edges of the stones of ancient ruins and sit in the crevices of their walls drinking water from a canteen. In the morning, as I listen to the birdsong, I wait for an inner stillness I have craved all my life. I want to feel, even if only for a moment, the fractured elements of who I am fall, finally, into place.

But the feeling never finds me.

I saw Roee again during my latest visit. After serving as a paratrooper during the Lebanese war, he had gone to college and then completed medical school. Although born into a secular American family, he had become very religious in Israel. When I opened Hagit's door after hearing his knock, I was greeted by a bearded man who wore a kipah on his head and tzitzit beneath his shirt. The tassels hung visibly at his waist. He was older and thinner than I remembered, but the face beneath the beard was that of my old friend; and the soft, gravelly voice speaking rapid Pittsburgh English was the same. But these days Roee spoke Hebrew in his daily life and lived in Jerusalem with his wife, Orna, and two of their three children. His eldest, a stepdaughter from Orna's first marriage, was in her twenties and living in Mount Hermon up north.

Having recently given up practicing medicine, Roee was working at a health care research firm in Tel Aviv and had transported his bicycle by bus that morning so he could ride it from work to Hagit's apartment. He accepted a warm hug, a sign that his Orthodoxy was at least somewhat flexible, and asked Hagit for the location of a kosher coffee shop. After listening to her directions, which were spoken in rapid Hebrew, we set out on foot to find it.

On Taiber Street, where Hagit has lived all her life, most of the buildings were built in the Bauhaus style, their facades constructed of unadorned cement. A woman pushed a stroller on the brick sidewalk beneath the ficus trees, and a couple holding hands passed by with clipped steps. A man stepped out of an apartment building followed by two boisterous children. When I walked with Hagit, such encounters inevitably led to a friendly "Shalom" and a brief exchange of news about family, work, or a recent vacation. Neighbors knew neighbors and were interested in each other's lives. In Boston, where I was living at the time of my visit, the neighbors on my street usually came and went without ever exchanging a word.

As Roee and I strolled, I noticed some activity in front of the Sephardic synagogue, a two-story, whitewashed cement building. A large pot filled with water had been set up on the sidewalk above a portable burner. Members of the congregation were stopping by with pots and pans that had to be boiled before Passover. According to Jewish tradition, used pots and pans must be boiled to make them kosher for use during the Passover week, when no leavened bread is allowed in the home. I saw one young man wearing blue jeans and sandals pull a few pots out of a backpack and hand them to an elderly, bearded man who was overseeing the boiling. After being raised in a country where lighting Christmas trees is such an integral part of life that many people consider it a national tradition, I never tired of witnessing the many Jewish customs that are incorporated into daily life in Israel.

Tel Aviv and its environs share a humid climate, unlike the parched Negev desert. In April, as the seasons transitioned from spring to summer, the air was damp and thick, although occasional rain offered relief from the humidity. It was warm and sunny at 5 PM when Roee and I arrived at the café, and we made our way to a small group of tables that had been set up on an outdoor patio in the back. Most Israelis speak at least some English, but communication flows easiest in Hebrew, so I deferred to Roee as he ordered coffee and two slices of apple cake. I had learned to speak Hebrew when I'd lived in Israel but never became fluent, and over the years my language skills had grown rusty. The step backward in comprehension was frustrating. In the past, speaking Hebrew had reinforced a sense of belonging. Now that I was struggling to communicate again I was keenly aware of a renewed alienation, and this seesaw mirrored the general experience of my life. I tended to arrive in a place, get my footing, work hard to find ways to connect and fit in, and then, once I had succeeded, move on.

Roee, on the other hand, was clearly at home. The waitress had placed the coffee and cake on our table, and we proceeded to talk for two hours. Our parents had been good friends as young couples in New York City, and because Roee and I were born just one day apart, we had played together as infants. No matter how many years went by between our meetings, the conversation flowed as if no time had passed. But this time thirteen years had gone by; and as we spoke, we realized that our lives, which had started in the same place, on almost the same day, could not have become more different. Roee, a religious doctor with a wife and three children, had been living in Israel for more than thirty years. His outlook was that of an Israeli; he had seen violence and war, and had the confidence Israelis exhibit in their eyes and their casual swagger. Life in Israel offers almost relentless opportunities for social connection as well as personal, intellectual, and religious discovery. But I don't think anyone would call life there easy, and Roee had developed that protective Israeli shell. But he also had the warm heart that so often lies beneath it.

As for me, I had spent one year of college studying in England and one year living in Israel, but the rest of my life has been spent in the United States. And in truth, I love America. I feel grateful that the United States gave my father's family a home after World War II when many countries closed their borders to Jewish refugees. Life in America offered my father numerous opportunities. He had access, most importantly, to an education that eventually led to a doctorate and a career as a successful psychotherapist. My mother's father worked in a shoe factory in New York City and married my grandmother, a gifted seamstress who had also escaped Europe before the war. With careful needlepoint, she created the golden badges that were sewn onto American military uniforms. Their children both attended college and earned advanced degrees; my uncle became a chemical engineer, and my mother worked in a biological research laboratory before beginning a career as a special education teacher. By the time my generation was born, the family was fully American; we played sports and watched TV, went to proms and drove cars, traveled, went to college, and started professional careers. My childhood friends came from varied backgrounds, and as an adult I have friends who immigrated to the United States from England, China, and Honduras. I feel rich as a human being because of the diversity that has become an integral part of my life.

Still, as I sat at a coffee shop in Givataim with Roee, I had to admit that he possessed a personal solidity that I had never known. He had thrown down his anchor long ago; and his family in Israel was deeply integrated into his religion, community, and country. We did share a number of things. We both had a nagging sense that by the age of forty-eight we should have achieved more professionally. We grappled with the knowledge that many of our youthful dreams about life and success might never be fulfilled. We had both experienced personal pain. But the foundation Roee felt beneath his feet was as enduring as the desert, while mine seemed to shift like the currents in the sea.

Finally it was time to go. We walked back to Hagit's apartment and said our good-byes in the narrow walkway where Roee had locked his bicycle to the railing. I felt sad as we parted, as if I were saying good-bye not only to an old friend, but also to the possibility of what my life might have been. We discussed whether we might meet again before I returned to the United States, but we both knew that such a meeting was unlikely.

"*L'hitraot*," I called after him as he rode away. The Hebrew phrase said at parting is a phrase of hope. See you again.

On my final morning in Israel, I watched through the bedroom window as the sun rose and turned the sky pink. I recorded the sound of the birds as they greeted the morning with song, then took a shower, finished packing, and shared breakfast with Hagit. I said good-bye to Ilan, Matan, and Talia, and hugged their white dog, Ketem, kissing the brown spot on his head. I followed Hagit downstairs and into their SUV. It was early, and the streets were nearly empty. As we left the city and drove toward the airport, I stared out the window and watched the flat, rocky landscape pass by. The nagging feeling that I was leaving my family behind disturbed me—not just Hagit's family, but also my first cousins and everyone in Israel who is related to me. I wished I could hand them passports that would provide access to the United States so they could escape the rockets and violence and uncertainty of this place.

But then I smiled to myself. Half my Israeli family already had American passports, and the other half didn't need or want them. Escape from Israel never crossed their minds; if anything, they wondered why I don't escape the uncertainty of life in the Diaspora. They loved this country, and the truth was, I loved it, too.

Hagit and I said good-bye in the crowded terminal with a hug, tears in our eyes. Two hours later, when I boarded my plane, I had no idea if I was leaving—or returning—home.

---

# CHAPTER SEVENTEEN

# The House on Amity Street

Rain hammers down onto Amity Street in the early morning, just before the first hint of light. The drops hit the pavement, burst like fireworks, then disappear. October is nearly over, and the sun takes its time rising in the distance and putting an end to the windy night. The street reveals itself in a slideshow of color: navy, powder blue, ghostly white with a tinge of pink, finally a steel-mill gray. The gray stage lingers as I glance up and down the street, wondering if we have lost any trees. But the hurricane has been relatively kind. Fallen leaves and broken branches are littered across lawns and plastered against houses. But the trees, like me, are still here—even though "here" is the last place I want to be.

I always bake too many cookies. Last night as the wind whipped through the trees and the Boston TV stations switched to emergency coverage, I prepared half the recipe that hangs on our refrigerator beneath a white magnet shaped like a KitchenAid mixer. My first husband kept the mixer itself; it was a wedding gift that we had both loved. I told myself that he should keep it because I was the one who had left.

It's an old habit: I give up what I want and settle for what I expect. Maybe this is how I ended up in a run-down house that was built in 1837. This is not a house I ever would have chosen. Located in the gritty Boston suburb of Waltham, both the structure itself and the lot that surrounds it were neglected for years. My second husband and I moved in after his mother had purchased the property as an investment. We steamed the yellowed wallpaper off the crumbling walls, pulled the shag carpets up from the floors, scrubbed the stains out of the blue ceramic bathtub, and painted over the racist graffiti inside the closet doors.

"I'll stay for five years," I said when I moved in.

Seven years later his mother is dead and we are still here.

Last night as I reached for the cookie ingredients, I noticed that the cream-colored paint on the kitchen cabinets is already wearing off. We hired a contractor who was really just a handyman to help us renovate the kitchen. We have discovered, over time, that he cut corners wherever possible. When he redid the floor, he left a layer of old linoleum beneath the new tile. Several of the tiles have already cracked. Sometimes when I see the cracks expanding, I want to grab a hammer and smash the whole floor to pieces.

It dips and rolls like the landscape of my childhood.

I was born against a backdrop of loss.

My mother's parents lost their homes and communities when they fled Eastern Europe before World War II. They found work in New York City's garment factories and raised a son and a daughter in a poverty-ridden section of the South Bronx.

My father's parents didn't make it out in time; they survived the Holocaust with three daughters and a son, but most of their community perished. After the war they made their way to New York City, where my father eventually met my mother.

I lived in Queens until I was six and my parents relocated to upstate New York. I attended classes in a three-room schoolhouse where I was the only child from the city and the only Jewish child in my grade. I made friends and adapted to my new surroundings, but despite everything my family had gained—the forty acres of hay fields that surrounded our house, the hills that rose to the sky beyond the fields, the maple trees with branches thick enough to hold tree houses, the pond we transformed into a skating rink every winter—we lived in a kind of void. It felt as if inside what we had found was what we had lost.

At seventeen I left home to attend Brandeis University, and that was when I first arrived in Waltham, Massachusetts. The university was located on a hill at the edge of town, separate from the rest of the community. I rarely ventured more than a few blocks from the campus, but my impression was that it was dirty, gray, and run-down—not a place where I would choose to live.

After completing a graduate program in Syracuse, I returned to the Boston area for a job. I was twenty-five, and I moved into the apartment in Waltham that my brother was vacating so I could have a place of my own. The rent was reasonable, and by continuing his lease I avoided paying a realtor's fee.

The apartment was on the first floor of an old rooming house, one block from the Main Street supermarket. The rooms were dark, the floors were scratched, and the wallpaper was peeling off the walls. The kitchenette smelled vaguely of gas, although the smell improved after the landlord replaced the stove that had been harboring not only a gas leak but a colony of cockroaches. I spent my days standing for up to an hour and a half on crowded commuter trains that were often delayed and rumbled along the tracks in and out of Boston. I met no one in Waltham except an elderly blind man who lived across the hall and asked me to read his mail to him.

When I left Waltham at twenty-eight to spend a year in Israel, I was sure that this time I would never return.

Thirteen years later a friend let me know that one of her colleagues needed a house sitter near Boston. I had been living like a nomad for more than a decade, searching for, but not finding, a place to call home. At loose ends, I accepted the offer.

The house, it turned out, was in Waltham.

Buddy and Grace, whose house is next door, have lived in Waltham for more than fifty years. Buddy is eighty-six and a man of small stature. He has a round face and blue, Irish eyes that twinkle with intelligence beneath his thinning white hair. Although he suffers from early onset Parkinson's, he still climbs a ladder to clean the gutters in the fall and mows the lawn with a push mower. He grows tomatoes and zucchini in a garden in their backyard, and shakes his head when he complains about the groundhog that regularly helps itself to his vegetables. But when he sees a worried look cross my face, he assures me with a shrug that he will let the "varmint" be.

Grace, at eighty-three, is vivacious, and frank, and a lover of neighborly conversation. I imagine she doesn't mind the wrinkles that line her face; after working in a factory that made weapons during World War II and raising five children who moved on long ago, she's not bothered by the minor things in life. Only the major things slow her down, like the colon cancer diagnosis three years ago that was followed by surgery and chemotherapy.

The doctors have told Grace that the cancer is gone, but she still hasn't regained all her energy. She has returned to walking to the supermarket to buy groceries, to painting and reading in her spare time, and to teaching a quilting class at the local senior center. But when she visits, I notice that her face seems paler.

The last time Grace stopped by, she arrived with a plastic bag filled with tomatoes from Buddy's garden. I invited her into our kitchen to talk for a while. Grace loves to tell stories about people who used to live on Amity Street. This time she described a woman who raised her family in the small yellow house that sits directly across from Buddy and Grace's. The woman used to cross the street to visit, accompanied by her children and the family's dog and cat. They approached the house as if lined up and marching in a parade, with the dog and cat trailing at the back. Grace laughed as she remembered the sight. Then her smile faded. After her children were grown, the woman left her husband and moved away.

"He was a terrible alcoholic, you see," Grace said, and our conversation paused.

"I think she's still alive," Grace added after a moment. "But I don't know. It's hard, you know, after someone moves away."

"Yes, it is," I said, and we both fell silent.

When I moved to Israel I had hoped to find what was lost before I was born. I spent the first six months in a study program located in a small town in the Negev desert. The program was housed in a quadrangle of cement dormitories at the southern edge of town. Just a short walk from the campus, across a neatly paved street, stood a stone wall that served as an overlook. Beyond the wall, the hills of the desert stretched for miles, pale and illusory beneath the blue sky. I used to sit on the wall and gaze at the endless panorama of ancient hills, their tawny slopes like the flanks of lionesses baking in the hot sun. The sight silenced me. The red line inside my mental speedometer fell to the left and stopped. I have experienced a similar stillness when surrounded by wilderness in other places: the fjords of Norway, the Rocky Mountains, the ocean as it crashes against the cliffs in Ireland, the unfathomable depths of Arizona's Grand Canyon.

I didn't find what I was looking for in Israel, but I found the kind of beauty that Waltham lacks. Here, from a footbridge that crosses the Charles River one block from our house, I see tires, rusty pipes, and discarded supermarket carts buried in brown mud beneath the water. To get to the footbridge I walk down a hill past a hodgepodge of houses and a redbrick apartment building with a badly overgrown lawn. Then I cross Lincoln Street, which is riddled with potholes, and follow a path between an industrial equipment warehouse and a tall chain-link fence reminiscent of the ones that guard prisons. The air has a vague odor of oil and gas. The walls of the warehouse are marked with graffiti; potato chip bags and beer cans lie in the underbrush.

My mind races when I walk in Waltham, while I look at the dirty river, until it finally settles on a single thought: *Out, out, I want out.*

The house on the other side of the street, at the top of the hill, belongs to a man who has lived in the neighborhood all his life. Joe is approaching sixty; his dark hair and mustache are sprinkled with gray. Although he recently survived a bad car accident, he still runs his own tree-trimming business.

Joe's garage is lined with ladders, saws, hammers, and a variety of other tools. We've discovered that he can build or fix anything. He has come to our rescue a number of times, lending us a tool when we needed one or explaining what piece had snapped and brought our snowblower suddenly to a halt. Once he lent us a ladder, a halter, and a climbing rope so Jean-Paul could remove an old clothesline pulley from a tree. The pulley, which had been installed long before we arrived, had been used to run a clothesline to our kitchen door. But when the house next to ours was sold to people we didn't know, we thought we should move the pulley onto our own property. Unfortunately the tree's bark had grown over the pulley, and we couldn't get it out of the tree.

I was leaning into the ladder, holding it steady while Jean-Paul balanced on top of it and hung from the halter off the tree. He was chipping around the pulley with a hammer and chisel when Joe strolled by with his six-year-old boxer, Jade. He stopped for a moment to watch and then said, "You know, you could just leave that pulley where it is and buy another one for ten bucks at the hardware store."

Three months ago Joe told me that Jade had suffered a seizure and died. I had just pulled into our driveway and was sitting in the driver's seat with the door open when Joe approached and told me the news. I sat there in shock, tears sliding down my face.

"It's just me and the turtle now," Joe said, referring to the small pet he keeps in his breezeway and lets out to wander around the yard every Sunday. "Yah, the turtle'll miss Jade; they were good pals," he added in that distinct Massachusetts drawl I can never imitate.

I watched as Joe walked slowly back to his house, his head down, hands stuffed into the pockets of his old jeans. Then I went inside and stood alone in our kitchen, not knowing how to handle my feelings of helpless grief. Eventually I opened one of the kitchen cabinets; pulled flour, sugar, and chocolate chips off a shelf; and started baking cookies.

People who live in Beverly Hills exist in a world I will never truly know. I had visited once, the year I turned forty, to spend time with a man I had dated in college. I'll call him Micah, which is not his real name. Micah grew up relatively poor, the son of two Holocaust survivors who had moved from Israel to New York City.

Micah hadn't been the greatest boyfriend in college; he cheated with other women and usually lied about the encounters. But perhaps because we had both grown up in the shadow of the Holocaust, the connection didn't end when the relationship did.

Micah earned a law degree, moved to Los Angeles, and eventually became a millionaire. When I saw him at forty, I was stunned by his surroundings: the ascending roads of the Hollywood hills, the gated mansions owned by celebrities, the view of the twinkling city at night from the hot tub on Micah's second-floor deck. Beverly Hills was a place I had a hard time reconciling with any other experience I'd ever had. It was beautiful, yes: the golden stone walls, the torches that lit the gates at night, the sleek black cars that pulled out of discreet driveways. I cannot deny that I envied, even coveted, this existence, this life of the privileged few. Micah took me to dinner on Rodeo Drive, and we watched the sun set from the deck of a boat he moored in the harbor at Marina del Ray.

But when I'd asked Micah, who had never married, what it was like to live in such a glorious place, to have this life that he worked hundred-hour weeks for fifteen years to achieve, he shrugged his shoulders and stared out at the darkening sky.

"The funny thing is, you're still you," he said.

Camila, who was born in Honduras, lives in the mustard-colored house with bloodred shutters that sits directly across the street from ours. She has lived in that house for thirty years, since she married the eldest son of the Italian family that owns it. Her husband, Alonzo, known by his American friends as Al, is fifty-six. When Al was a child in Italy, his six-year-old sister was shot and killed by a neighbor's boy who was playing with a gun. Al's devastated parents eventually left Italy, taking Al to Venezuela and then to the United States, where they eventually had a second son. They purchased the house in Waltham, which had a large Italian population at the time, and separated it into apartments to accommodate Al and his brother, Fillipo. Fillipo eventually moved out, but Al remained and still lives in the house. His father used to knock on our door and present us with paper bags full of pears harvested from the trees that grew in their yard. Several years ago the old man had a stroke and died. In his anguish, Al cut down the trees.

Camila came to the United States when she was in her early twenties; her father died of cancer in Honduras before she could get back to see him. At fifty-three she is five foot four and wears skin-tight blouses and jeans. She has dark eyes and wavy, shoulder-length hair that she dyes a copper blond. Camila works as an accountant at a hospital during the day and behind the desk at the local gym four evenings a week. She laughs easily and often, and when I cross the street to visit, she grabs my arm and pulls me upstairs to her living room, where we sip cheap rosé and eat crackers and cheese. The room is lined with knickknacks: ceramic animals, snow globes, black-and-white photos from Honduras, souvenirs from driving trips to Disney World. A large wooden cross hangs from one of the walls. In the bedroom hangs a painting Al once did of Jesus.

Camila lowers her voice when she tells me conspiratorially about her many experiences communing with spirits. She has seen Al's father quite a few times since his death and recently heard Fillipo, who died of cancer, knock on her door in the middle of the night. She has seen images of Jesus and the Virgin in the sky or in patches of light on the walls. She shows me photographs as proof; and when I look carefully at the photos without saying a word, she says, "I know that you don't…" but then stops. She expects me to laugh, and to tell her that I don't believe in Jesus and that none of this can be true.

But I never say this. I remain silent. Camila continues, "Anyway, it's all one God."

I see the faces in her photos.

"I'll run across the street and give them to you. Just come downstairs and open your door."

I was trying to convince Camila to take some of the cookies I had baked last night during the hurricane.

"You are crazy!" she said, laughing into the phone. "The wind is really bad, and I don't want to go out."

"Just come downstairs and open your door. I'll bring them to you."

"You can't do that! There's so much water!" she replied, laughing again.

"I'm coming over now. Open your door."

I wrapped a pile of cookies in aluminum foil. Racing across the street, I had to bend my head forward and hold the hood of my raincoat to protect my face from the wind. Camila opened her door. She was wearing a coat she had thrown over her pajamas.

"You are crazy!" she said again as I shoved the cookies into her hands before darting back across the street. I pulled open the door and fell back into the house before slamming it shut behind me.

In the farmhouse of my youth, life emerged as a blend of normalcy and pain. We ate dinner, cleaned our rooms, did homework, watched television. But my father, when he was home from his four-day workweek in the city, was often angry or depressed. My mother maintained the house on her own. She made few friends. My brother, who is two years older than me, shut himself in his room and played loud music on his stereo. I argued with my sister, who was born in Korea and adopted by my parents when we were both five years old. Out of an anger I didn't understand at the time, I teased her, calling her by her Korean name: Eun. She responded by chasing me through the house. Once she kicked a hole in the door of the bathroom where I was hiding.

I knew my parents loved me, and I excelled when I was busy at school. But I felt trapped when I was inside our secluded farmhouse, where the pain seemed to hang with the cobwebs in dark corners. In fact, I can't remember many moments when I was actually inside the house.

I do remember staring out the windows. The fields stretched and rolled toward the hills. Turkey vultures and red-tailed hawks sailed in the sky. At twilight, white-tailed deer emerged from the woods, pricking their ears and searching for food.

Two black-gray tabbies we adopted from a nearby farm trotted across the yard.

An orange tabby with white paws, a white breast, and a red collar sometimes drifts toward our house on Amity Street. I have noticed him sitting near a cluster of houses at the corner of James and Howland, one block over at the top of the hill. Occasionally he makes his way into our backyard to sniff around the feeding station I used to maintain for feral cats.

The feeding station, a small wooden structure with a shingled roof, was supplied by a local rescue organization. I called them three years ago to report that I had seen a cat with four kittens in our yard. When I first moved onto Amity Street, a colony of homeless cats roamed freely around the neighborhood. Initially I didn't realize that the cats had no homes; I thought some neighbors let their pets wander outdoors, a choice that I now consider dangerous. But I noticed that these cats were wiry, and thin, and sometimes very dirty. When I spotted a small female squeezing her kittens through a gap in the fencing beneath our back deck, I could no longer rationalize inaction.

The Cat Connection runs a trap/neuter/release program designed to protect and maintain feral colonies. The group sent a volunteer to my house to determine if the kittens I had spotted might be young enough to be tamed for adoption. Deb, the volunteer, was about my age, medium height, blond hair, and blue eyes. She arrived in a utilitarian sweatshirt and jeans, and had a businesslike, no-nonsense attitude. She clearly had seen too many cats on the streets. Her Volvo station wagon was loaded with steel traps, old blankets, and large bags of dry cat food. I didn't know at the time that Deb has a law degree and teaches courses at a local university while running a cage-free cat shelter full-time.

Deb taught me how to feed the cats at regular intervals until they could be tempted by the food to enter the humane traps. Once trapped, they would be fixed, vaccinated, and tested for disease. Kittens young enough to tame, along with strays that had clearly had homes at some point, would be placed in foster homes and put up for adoption. My commitment, in exchange for these free services, was to feed any older cats that were returned to our yard if it was determined that they were too wild to tame.

We trapped a dozen cats, including six kittens, and only four were returned to our yard. Over the next three years I managed to tame all the cats who returned except a small white female who wouldn't come near me. One cat disappeared before I could retrap him, but another was successfully adopted. A large gray-and-white tom called Franklin moved in with us and became a deeply loved pet. Franklin had a scar on his upper lip, ears that had been chewed up and torn in fights, a tooth infection, and a polyp in his ear canal. We got him the veterinary care he needed, and once he understood that he now had a home, he stuck to us like glue every minute.

I was uncomfortable with the idea of letting Franklin go back outside, but sometimes we let him out to see the little white female. She had followed Franklin everywhere when he lived outdoors and had been heartbroken when he seemed to disappear. Some cats have a tendency to form bonded pairs, and this female had bonded with Franklin. She used to stare through our kitchen window, hoping to see him.

Finally we let Franklin outside for a visit, and the little white cat danced around him and rolled joyfully in the grass. I was uneasy whenever he went out, but he stayed within the confines of our yard, only occasionally slipping behind the back fence to sniff around a neighbor's toolshed.

One rainy morning Franklin ran out the kitchen door when I opened it to place food out for the little female. I thought he would return immediately once he realized it was raining, but, uncharacteristically, he ran directly to the back of the yard where the white female waited and disappeared with her under the fence. A minute later I heard what sounded like a puppy crying out behind the fence. I ran out and stopped dead when I saw, to my astonishment, a coyote standing a few feet away from me in the yard. I yelled at the coyote, "Go!" and as it disappeared toward Amity Street, I squeezed through an opening in the fence and saw Franklin lying on the ground with blood on his neck. He was alive but gasping for breath.

The next thing I remember is racing through the streets of Waltham in my car with Franklin lying beside me on the passenger seat, bleeding. I steered with my left hand and kept my right hand on Franklin's flank so he would know I was there. I ran every red light between our house and the emergency veterinary hospital ten minutes away. My breath came so fast and shallow that I thought I might hyperventilate. I cried, "Please, God, please God," out loud over, and over.

It was 6:45 on the morning of July fourth. God wasn't listening.

Franklin is buried in the backyard of our house on Amity Street. And now as I sit at the desk in my upstairs writing room, the little white female crouches in the corner behind me. It took weeks to tempt her through the open back door with plates of her favorite food. One day after she ventured inside, I closed the door behind her. For seven years I have dreamed of breaking out of these damn walls, yet I wanted her safely inside them.

Lamplight glows in two windows across the street. The only sound I hear when I open the window is the distant hum of traffic on the Massachusetts Turnpike. One mile away commuters are driving into Boston, even at this hour. Taxis are headed to the airport, where their passengers will catch the first morning flights to their next destination.

I think about my neighbors who have lived on Amity Street for thirty, forty, fifty years. I think of how they live, and cry, and mourn, and die. They plant their gardens, walk their turtles, and sometimes see Jesus in a light or in the sky. There is nothing else they can do.

I rescue cats and bake cookies. There is nothing else I can do.

For so long I have wanted to get out of this decrepit house. For so long I have dreamed of escape from this town. Yet here I am, where the river is polluted and the streets are paved with loss, watching it get battered by the rain after a hurricane.

Why am I still here?

Because the house on Amity Street is like any other house, even those big, pretty mansions in Beverly Hills. And Waltham is the same as the desert or the mountains or the ocean or any other place. You can't drown loss in a landscape. But by sharing it with neighbors who have always understood this, I am as safe from the pain here as I would be anywhere.

# CHAPTER EIGHTEEN

# Let Go

The woman behind me is drunk. She leans toward me, shouting to be heard above the music that screams from the speakers on the stage.

"The blond one is cute, eh?" she yells into my ear, her comment punctuated by that charming Canadian "eh?" She's talking about David Victor, one of the guitarists for the band Boston. I glance over my shoulder and smile at her briefly before returning my attention to the stage. The music is so loud that there are moments when I wonder if my ears might begin to bleed, and I stick my fingers inside to protect them. My gut vibrates with every beat of the bass drum.

David Victor is standing on the other side of the stage, wailing on a Gibson Les Paul. He is cute. The music flows from his fingers through the frets of his guitar as if the instrument is an extension of his body. His shoulder-length blond hair is slick with sweat, his slim chest hugged by a sleeveless black t-shirt. His jeans are appealingly tight. I consider all this with my husband standing just a few feet behind me in the crowd, his eyes on the stage, his hands stuffed into the pockets of his shorts. I smile to myself. I am forty-nine and married but I'm certainly not dead, and at this moment I am convinced that the reason men were put on Earth was to play rock-and-roll music in a band.

More than eight thousand people are crammed into Harris Park at the edge of the Thames River in London, Ontario. It is 2012, and the sun has just set on the last Saturday night in July. The clouds that blew over the city have moved on and taken any remnants of rain with them. The air is warm and damp, the ground is muddy, and the indigo sky is fading to black. Happy Canadians have been listening to warm-up bands, eating shawarma and kebobs, and drinking beer since four o'clock. "It's an old-fashioned rock festival!" George Thorogood declared joyfully in the middle of his performance last night.

I bought tickets to "Rock the Park" a few months ago after noticing the event listed online. A trip to Canada for a classic rock concert seemed like the perfect celebration for an upcoming milestone: Jean-Paul's fiftieth birthday. Jean-Paul's heritage is French Canadian, his passion is the guitar, and the first musician he saw play live was none other than George Thorogood. The concert was scheduled just a few days before his birthday. I bought tickets for a JetBlue flight from Boston to Buffalo, reserved a rental car, mapped a route that would take us through Niagara Falls, and booked a room at the concert's sponsoring hotel. A month working an extra temp job paid for the trip.

I hang both arms over the metal barrier in front of me and hold on tight. A man dancing behind me bumps into my back and pushes me forward against the barrier. I can't feel annoyed. The man's hair is pure white, his face is red with drink, and his smile radiates happiness. He is excited and having a good time. A woman standing next to him grabs the barrier with her hand and tries to pull her body closer to the stage. But if I give even an inch I will lose my place in the front row, and for once in my life I am not stepping aside. Not for this woman, who is clearly determined but is also self-absorbed, and not, frankly, for anyone. I worked in the music business for a few years in the 1990s, and I have had my share of good seats and backstage passes. But I have never before stood in the front row at a concert, where nothing but a barrier and a few security guards separate the crowd from the stage. One of my favorite bands is performing just a few feet in front of me, and I am determined, just once, to stand so close that I can see the musicians' faces and watch their fingers fly up and down the frets of their guitars. I could almost reach out and touch them. But I get rattled when the crowd behind me presses forward, and for the most part I don't look back. Thankfully only a few hundred people with VIP tickets have access to this area near the stage.

The band, by design, is staying faithful to the arrangements of Boston's major hit songs from the 1970s and 1980s. When the musicians clap their hands above their heads while looking out at the crowd, the audience responds with a happy roar, claps along with the beat, and shouts lyrics back at the band. They remember every word, every note, that accompanied a romance or road trip, a lost dream, a moment of hope or despair.

This is one of the moments when I feel no despair. I have been told that one of the advantages of oversensitivity is that while you are capable of feeling pain to unfathomable depths, you can also experience immeasurable joy. And joy is what I feel right now, a jubilation that courses through my body and prevents me from lingering on any single thought. Everything lifts, even the image of my father having trouble rising from the couch, and the empty streets that stretch in front of my car as I run a red light in the early morning with one hand resting on my bleeding, dying cat. The face of the coyote who stood confused in our backyard no longer haunts me. Arguments with Jean-Paul disintegrate. No. None of that is invited to join me here. The music engulfs my pain and spits it back out, splintering and spinning it like colors in a kaleidoscope until it is transformed into something achingly beautiful.

It strikes me that I feel happy as an alien here. This moment is not taking place in the small town where I was raised or even in the country where I was born. Behind me is a crowd of perfect strangers. The only person I know in this park is my husband, and even he exists in a world apart from mine, absorbed in the musical concepts that inspire each note, in ideas that I don't fully understand.

I am alone here, in front of eight thousand people. And tonight, just right now, it's okay. The place that I come from and the road I have traveled don't matter. The only thing that is important is that I have arrived here, now, in the midst of a collective consciousness. And although I am alone, I can sense that I share this time and place, this era that is and has been my life. It will all fade like fame. Glory days. The things that linger, like desire or a beloved soul, only to perish someday.

I let go of the barrier and dance.

# How This Book Came to Be
# (As Told on Facebook)

*March 24, 2009*

Contractor + roofer + hammers + dust = Panera

*March 26, 2009*

Faye's life: Bring laptop to Panera to escape the hammering and sawing at home. Buy coffee, low-fat muffin. Sit down, open laptop. Watch a school bus pull up to the curb and unload an explosion of thirty middle-school students, who stream into Panera and turn the place into Grand Central Station.

*March 30, 2009*

Sitting next to six elderly men talking at the next table. One is wearing a U.S. Army veteran's hat, and I get the sense they are WWII veterans. A silent "thanks" from me to them.

*April 2, 2009*

I am so happy that the woman who sat down next to me and proceeded to hum the entire time has left.

*April 3, 2009*

Panera Chronicles: If you drop part of your low-fat blueberry muffin on the floor, do you still have to count all 360 calories?

*April 7, 2009*

Sitting in "laptop corner," where lone computer users glance furtively at each other before quickly looking back at their screens, glaring with annoyance at people who talk at other tables.

*April 14, 2009*

It's official: I'm a Panera regular. The man who works at the counter every morning recognized me today. He stamped my "frequent coffee card" three times, instead of one, to give me a head start on a free cup of coffee.

*April 24, 20009*

Back in Panera's "laptop corner," near the group of WW II veterans...and the University of Rochester women's tennis team, who just arrived by bus. They must be in Boston for a match. Happiness is a free cup of coffee, thanks to the extra stamps on my card courtesy of the man at the counter.

*April 25, 2009*

Joy, joy, joy, sun, sun, sun

*April 27, 209*

Rejections, rejections, rejections

*May 4, 2009*

Spin class: I went, I spun. Then I drove myself to Panera and ate a pumpkin muffie.

*June 4, 2009*

Can the Muses be heard at Panera?

*June 11, 2009*

Just heard a member of the WWII veterans' group say that today is his 83rd birthday.

*August 21, 2009*

Listening to the WW II veterans talk about being in the army at 18, and describing their memories of the Germans.

*August 26, 2009*

You try to be good by ordering the 240-calorie pumpkin muffie at Panera. The guy behind the counter insists that you sample not one, not two, not three, but four pieces of their new chocolate macadamia nut brownies. "Use your hands! This is like home, for God's sake," he says.

*September 4, 2009*

Listening to the WW II veterans talk at their table. One just said that his parents wouldn't sign his permission form when he tried to enlist at 17 because he was the oldest child and they needed him. Another said his parents signed the form right away because they couldn't wait to get rid of him.

*September 11, 2009*

Reading and typing in English, while two women at the table to my left yammer in French. My mind is switching back and forth between the two languages and feels like it's going to explode.

*September 11, 2009*

A friend of mine was digging for survivors in the rubble after the World Trade Center fell on September 11, 2001. He found a stuffed bear from a gift shop that was probably located at the top of one of the towers. He gave the bear to me, and I treasure it. It has the words "Top of the World, World Trade Center" stitched onto the front.

*October 9, 2011*

Sipping a cup of hazelnut coffee, sitting near the World

War II veterans, staring at my computer screen, and thinking: "Back to the drawing board."

*October 24, 2010*

Note to self: Panera is a lot more crowded and noisy on the weekend, especially when it's raining.

*October 26, 2009*

Thinking about a stretch of road I drove this morning on the way to Panera. Yellow and orange leaves ablaze on the trees, glowing in the morning sunshine. My mind went blank for a moment—it was so beautiful.

*November 10, 2009*

At Panera early, before 9 this morning. It's interesting how the culture changes by the hour. The World War II veterans haven't arrived yet, but a large group of utility workers were just here, taking up a few tables, and quietly having coffee before the start of their workday.

*November 11, 2009*

Happiness is when the counter guy at Panera has your coffee mug ready before you even get to the front of the line. (P.S. On the lookout for the World War II veterans, because I want to buy *their* coffee on Veteran's Day.)

*November 17, 2009*

Sitting at Panera listening to the early morning clatter of dishes and thinking about an email I received from an ex-boyfriend I haven't seen in eight years.

*November 30, 2009*

"Crisis" this morning. I set up my laptop at a table at Panera, ordered my mug of coffee and pumpkin muffie, and then sat down to discover the free Wi-Fi wasn't working. What will I do? Oh, right. Write.

### December 2, 2009

Contemplating this strange little blue gadget I have to live with for two and a half months until my AT&T contract allows me to get a new iPhone without going broke. The gadget is called a "cell phone," and all it does is make phone calls. I think fondly of the typewriter (remember those?).

### December 16, 2009

Back at Panera, where the fellow who always remembers me is at the counter with my warm cup of hazelnut coffee, and encouraging notes from Facebook friends nudge the blues away.

### December 23, 2000

Sitting at Panera surrounded by jazzy Christmas music and the noisy conversations going on around me, trying to figure out why teenagers wear bedroom slippers as shoes.

### January 27, 2010

Thankfully, the woman who was talking and laughing so loudly at the next table has left Panera. Don't people know that coffee shops are for writing, not for drinking, eating, and laughing with friends? Wait…

### February 25, 2010

I have been sitting at Panera for the last couple of hours, writing on my laptop. An elderly gentleman who has been sitting nearby just turned to me and said, "If I had a laptop, I'd send you a nice email."

### March 9, 2010

Watching the World War II veterans trickle in for their morning coffee. I spoke to one of the women, and she said that her daughter was one of the first female Navy pilots. She lands her plane on aircraft carriers. Meanwhile, the fellow at the table in front of me has been holding a video camera near his ear for an hour, listening carefully. The next great documentary?

*March 30, 2010*

Rain, rain, rain.

*April 28, 2010*

Write, write, write.

*April 30, 2010*

Listening to one of the World War II veterans at the next table tell a young man about his experiences as a gunner in Europe. He just mentioned a very cold winter and the Battle of the Bulge.

*May 7, 2010*

World War II veterans collected for coffee at the next table, laptops open on tables, people tapping on keyboards, piano jazz playing softly in the background.

*May 19, 2010*

Panera is crowded on this rainy Boston day. A man just walked in with a huge pile of files, stuffed manila envelopes, and notebooks, and set them all down on the next table before walking off to order something. Panera: the new office.

*June 15, 2010*

Working/writing at Panera, where my favorite counter guy had my mug waiting, and explained how he puts together the yogurt, fruit, and granola cups. He told me that the pumpkin muffie has less calories and fat than the yogurt (what a shame).

*July 25, 2010*

Oh restless thoughts, we are old friends.

*August 23, 2010*

A moment when it's nice to be in the U.S.: a Latino man

walks into the coffee shop with his wife, and orders two bagels, toasted.

A moment when I wonder about the U.S.: I turn on my laptop and a news headline reads: "Cupcake Fight on The Kardashians."

*September 16, 2010*

Dunkin' Donuts today, because I'm waiting for my car to be fixed nearby. Hide a tear after reading a short essay about the sighting of a bird that had been presumed extinct. "Kung Fu Fighting" starts playing over the PA. Two black stretch limos drive slowly through the gritty parking lot. "Sister Golden Hair" starts playing: "Will you love me just a little, just enough to show you care?"

*October 26, 2010*

A round, older woman who works at Panera just wiped off the table next to mine, noticed me sitting cross-legged and typing, and said, "You look just like a college kid sitting there, a college kid doing her homework. Good girl." I was working on an essay about the pain of lost youth. Thank you, universe, for small favors.

*November 11, 2010*

I bought a round of coffee for the World War II veterans who gather at Panera every morning. "Thank you" can never be said enough.

*November 23, 2010*

Early morning at Panera, jazz playing over the loudspeakers. A young man with Down syndrome talks excitedly about his favorite team with someone in line who is wearing the team's logo on a jacket. The staff helps the young man sign up for a My Panera card, informs him that he will receive a free cinnamon roll. He happily orders two.

*December 7, 2010*

The World War II veterans chat and laugh at a nearby table cluttered with coffee mugs and food trays. Two wear army hats, three wear Irish tweed caps. Two still have their winter jackets on. It's 30 degrees outside, but we're all warm in here.

# *Acknowledgments*

**With gratitude:**

~ To Joy Castro, without whose mentoring and friendship I would not be the writer I am today.

~ To Michael Steinberg, who has given more time to my work than I had a right to expect, and who has inspired me to keep writing through the toughest times.

~ To Laban Carrick Hill, who inspires me always.

~ To Jean-Paul, for more than words can say.

~ To Randall Kenan, Ray Gonzalez, and Amy Hoffman, whose teaching at the Solstice MFA Program in Creative Writing at Pine Manor College helped me develop my work and reach new heights as a writer.

~ To MaryChris Bradley, for her belief in my work and her acceptance of this manuscript.

~ To my wonderful agent, Joan Schweighardt, for always believing in me and in my work, and for encouraging me to complete this manuscript.

~ To my tireless, enthusiastic, keen-eyed proofreader and friend Lori Groudas, who spent countless hours reading, and rereading, my work.

~ To Melissa Varnavas and Cindy Zelman, who provided comments on early drafts of some of the individual essays included in this book.

~ To Kerry Beckford and Chris Daly, who provided so much help during my first semester as a college writing instructor —a job that improved my own writing.

˜ To Meg Kearney, Tanya Whiton, and the many students and teachers I met through the Solstice MFA Program at Pine Manor College.

˜ To all the literary journal editors who published individual essays from this collection.

˜ To Peggy Dey, whose lifelong friendship inspired some of the writing in this book.

˜ To Amy Porter, for giving me "carte blanche."

˜ To Jill Agostino, for her friendship and for offering me the opportunity to write for *The New York Times*.

˜ To Naomi Kirshner, for being "Nao."

˜ To Rachel Donovan Vigil and Arthur Vigil, for their friendship and support.

˜ To Alvita Liktorius Barsky, for her friendship.

˜ To the triumvirate in Boston: Beth Glick, and Amy and Howie Zuckerman.

˜ To Aaron Pearlman, for standing by me during some of the most difficult times in my life.

˜ To my cats, who were—and are—always by my side.

˜ To my beloved family.

CPSIA information can be obtained at www.ICGtesting.com
Printed in the USA
LVOW13s0424190514

386366LV00003B/115/P